ABORIGINALITIES

Royal Museums
of Fine Arts of Belgium

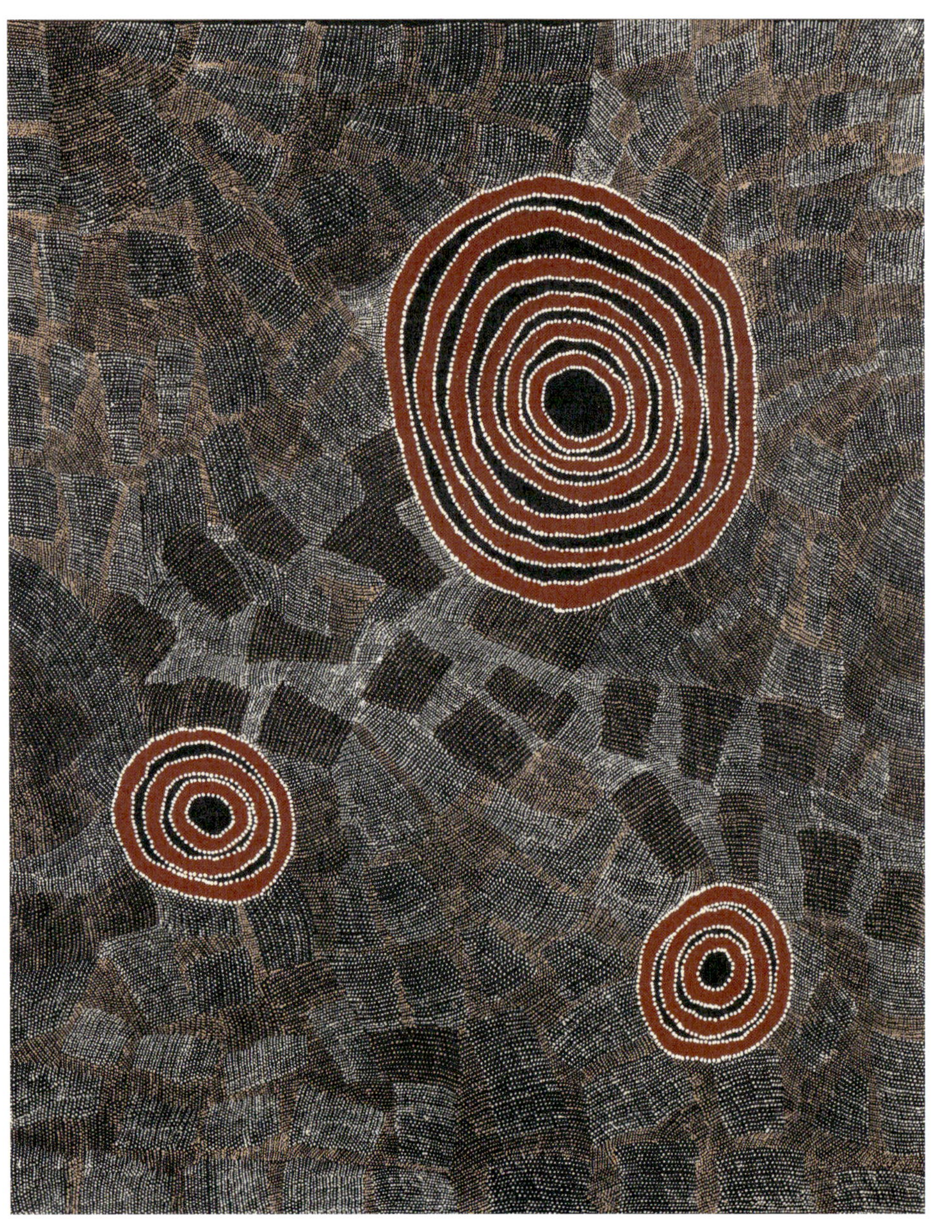

Wentja Morgan Napaltjarri – *Rockhole West of Kintore*, 2015

Acrylic on canvas, 152 × 122 cm, Philippson Collection

INTRODUCTION

MICHEL DRAGUET

The "Aboriginalities" exhibition was put together from a collection of around 260 works collected by Marie Philippson. Over some twenty years, this prominent figure from the Brussels cultural scene has focused on works that are more about personal taste, based on a certain idea of modernity, than a desire to compile an exhaustive picture of Aboriginal art in its regional or stylistic diversity.

The term "aboriginality" stems from an "abori**ge**nality" asserted as early as the 1950s by the indigenous people of the southern continent. "Aboriginal" is a term coined by settlers to exclude the original peoples, who were deprived of rights and identity, to the benefit of "Australians" who saw themselves as the first occupants of a country perceived as *terra nullius*: nobody's land. The aim is to assert — and thus display — a cultural identity that restores a sense of existence to the first peoples of the southern continent, on which any political, social, and economic struggles to assert an aboriginal reality are based: languages, social practices (including extremely complex modes of filiation), visions of the world ingrained in the "Dreamtime", artistic creations, the relationship to nature as something which embodies the individual, transmission of ancient knowledge, rituals, and ceremonies... All these elements play a part in the construction of an identity marked by this *aborigenality* and have led to the recognition of their claims to "land rights", which marked the advent of an aboriginal nation.

Aborigenality becomes *abori**gi**nality* by stepping out of the Australian context to enter a contemporary Western debate. The neologism "aboriginality" reflects this view which, between here and elsewhere, between self and other, defines reciprocity nurtured by expectations. Thus, *aboriginality* reflects, on one hand, the aspiration to primitivism inherent to the late and early 20th century that no longer speaks of "primitive" (a term now rejected for its pejorative connotations), but instead, of Western modernity that, in order to break with the norms inherited from humanism, needed a combination of savagery and fantasised childhood in the prehistoric past and in the exotic elsewhere.

Yet *aboriginality* is not an updated form of primitivism. It is also a desire to place the future on a different trajectory from the path of modernity: a return to Gaia through the consecration of nature threatened by destruction, a desire to go back in time, to relive an era of imagined harmony, an urge to recreate intimacy with the world by breaking away from the dogmas of free trade and capitalism, a desire to unshackle oneself from the tyranny of finance and business as a means to rediscover knowledge that would have been lost for want of initiated people...

However, *aborigenality* can pose a threat if it is perceived as a form of essentialism that only addresses the — inevitably original — purity of the aboriginal state. Anthropologist Clifford James demonstrated that cultures subjected to contact with Westerners could not go back in time to a past perceived as Edenic or ideal. To be active, *aborigenality* must embrace this place in history, which *necessarily* culminates in a form of cultural hybridity: a space for dialogue, for exchange, for becoming, driven not by the frustrations of history, but by a desire to build something together. This is what *aboriginality* refers to, not least by including an awareness of "modernity".

In the Australian context of a resurging Aboriginal identity marked by political, social, and economic struggles, this "modernity" was articulated in 1971 when Geoffrey Bardon (1940–2003), a young community leader based in the Papunya settlement, invited the elders to "translate" their cultural practices and initiatory knowledge into paintings. Thus, the Papunya Tula workshop became a laboratory for a form of expression perpetuating Aboriginal traditions such as bark painting, which is widespread in Arnhem Land in the Northern Territories. The artform quickly proved popular with Australian galleries and government authorities, which were facing a change in public opinion about the Aboriginal issue. Aboriginal painting soon became an "official" movement with its own scrupulously analysed and documented value; it is now an international gold standard. Biennials, galleries, and other art fairs give pride of place to these artists who express an ancestral past in ways that rival the work of the best-known Western artists. In so doing, they have enabled the accomplishment of the initial project underlying Papunya Tula's "revolution": to express an age-old cultural identity hitherto unrecognised by Australians, using Western means (acrylics, brushes, cardboard, and then canvas) and to rescue the indigenous people of the Australian continent from a state of non-existence that they had endured since colonisation.

There is no doubt that this "echo strategy" remains one of the most outstanding forms of cultural hybridisation of the 20th century. By welcoming Aboriginal artists to a Museum of "Fine Arts", a flagship of Western cultural identity, we hope to encourage similar interactions with our own collections. First, with the work of Pierre Alechinsky, who was deeply inspired by an ethnographic sensitivity acquired through his association with Asger Jorn and within Cobra. Then with a selection of paintings, drawings, and sculptures drawn from our collections to illustrate *modern* creation, beyond the aberrations of the concept of "*aboriginality*".

Some visitors will doubtless interpret this exhibition as a return to the formalist discourse that dominated the 1984 exhibition "Primitivism and Modern Art" held at the Museum of Modern Art in New York. A form of primitivism to be understood not as an attempt to define so-called "primitive" civilisations, but as its instrumentalisation by Western creation in its quest for forms of expression that would effectively release it from its own tradition. Others might find an echo of the 1989 exhibition "Magiciens de la Terre" presented at the Centre Georges Pompidou, where Richard Long's *Red Earth Circle* was installed just behind the Yuendumu community's *Yam Dreaming*, an aboriginal sand carpet.

The Philippson collection stands at this crossroads. Mindful of progressivism and modernism, and sensitive to the intersection between cultures, Marie Philippson and her husband and accomplice Alain have found the essence of this form of aspiration in Australian Aboriginal painters. It is far from the essentialism that refers to the ethnographic viewpoint or the primitivism that has shrouded Aboriginal culture for the past century in a fantasised, primeval guise at the frontier of childhood, savagery, and madness. Instead, the knowledge gained from Marie Philippson's peregrinations relentlessly calls for this hybridisation, which defines the progress of cultures and individuals in their encounters with others as a condition for their own personal development.

The knowledge gained from anthropology lends its fundamental sense to a style of painting whose power is firmly rooted in the contemporary moment. The survival of an initial world — or, more precisely, of this "Dreamtime" which is the basis of a cosmogony — only finds meaning in its continuous reactivation, in the social, cultural, economic, and political sense. Thus, Aboriginals provide the opportunity for contemporary creation to shed its cold intellectualism by recasting the modernist project on the foundations of a return to the constituent act of the universe. In this way, *aboriginality* builds a new universality whose centre of gravity is outside the West.

In an era where intercultural dialogue and exchanges are giving way to fragmentation and radicalisation, the marginalisation of "another" culture by a globalised, i.e. Westernised, market can be questioned; its exploitation can be decried as an extension of colonialism; every form of appropriation can be stigmatised, and the most extreme positions of "political correctness" can be caricatured. It could also be seen as the expression of a community of destinies linking the "Whitefella" to the Aborigine, the Western artist to the third-generation painter, for whom ritual experiences no longer have the same importance as they did for the early pioneers of Papunya Tula.

Our approach is not intended to establish a formal link between the productions of one culture with those of another, nor is it meant to assert the superiority of one over the other. Quite the contrary, the juxtaposition simply attempts to create "intersecting zones" where the issues tackled in the field of Aboriginal painting offer a new perspective to the same questions that pervade Western art. For instance, the feminine aspect of recent Aboriginal painting is a case in point. This approach will inevitably raise questions about our Western situation and the vestiges of patriarchy.

With some 130 artworks, we invite you to discover — through the art of the indigenous people of Australia — this *aboriginality* that addresses our place and our future on Gaia, our Mother Earth. Without seeking to find clear-cut and absolute answers, but simply to enjoy a feeling of closeness that represents — who knows? — the premonition of an awakening to this now much-maligned universality.

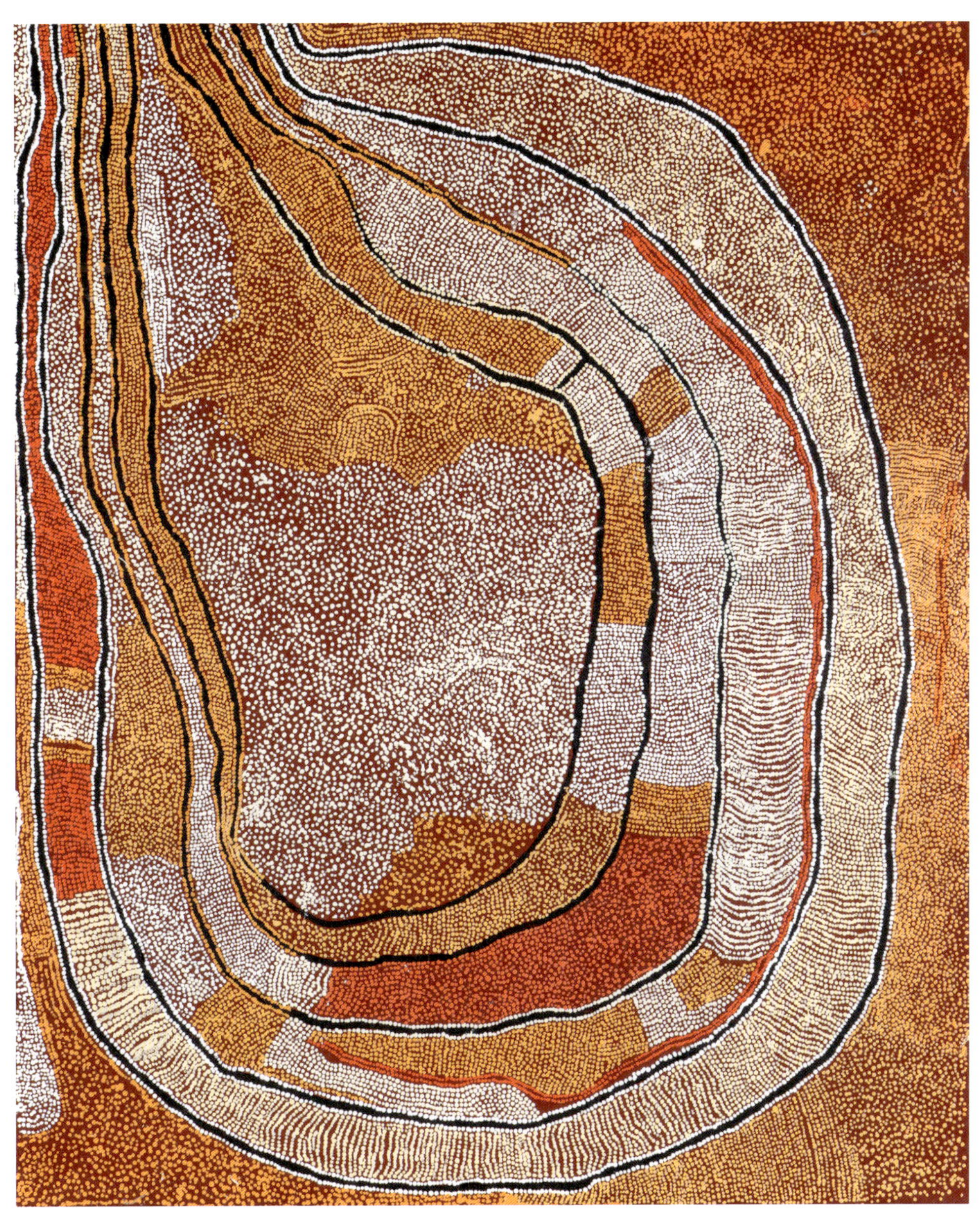

Naata Nungurrayi – *Marrapinti*, 2005
Acrylic on canvas, 182 × 152 cm, Philippson Collection

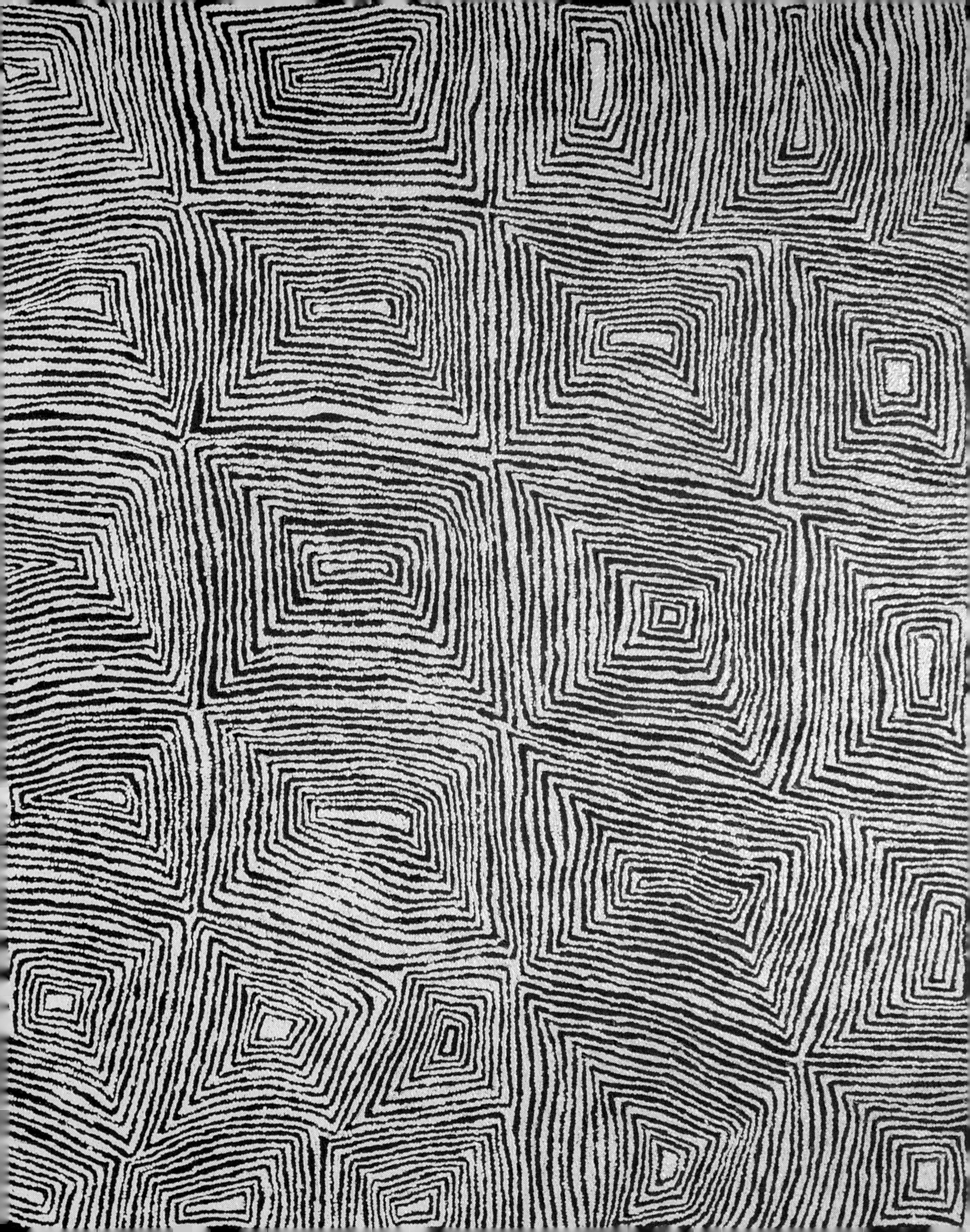

FIVE KEY CONCEPTS TO UNDERSTAND ABORIGINAL ART

Clan — The clan plays an essential role in the structure of Aboriginal society. It is made up of a group of individuals who recognise themselves as belonging to the same bloodline (patrilineal, matrilineal, or in relation to an Ancestor, shared spirit or even a totemic reference figure). The individual is not the norm and lineages can be duplicated depending on where the individual is anchored in the community. In a number of regions, land rights and the organisation of rituals (including paintings) fall under the authority of clans.

Parentage — The Aboriginal filiation system is one of the most complicated to study anywhere in the world. Kinship can be patrilineal or matrilineal and is organised in halves: in itself, the society is divided into two halves, according to which the rules of marriage are structured. The parentage system is also organised into sections and sub-sections. Every individual belongs to a group divided into four sections and eight subsections. The name of the sub-section is typically used as a surname in the usual sense. Kinship also involves Ancestor spirits, based on emblematic places of the Dreamtime. These spirits contribute to the concept of the individual by connecting them to totemic entities.

Thus, from halves to subsections, by way of the Ancestor spirit attached to a place where his "genius" is still active, the individual is not only identified by his genetic descent, but also by a network of ritual and symbolic connections that place him within a multiplicity of groups.

For indigenous Australians, the individual is linked to the Ancestor; on the one hand, through a genealogical link with the spirit of the place which fertilised the pregnant woman; on the other hand, through the continued presence of the Ancestor in the landscape that he created by naming it. A spiritualistic conception of the universe is thus drawn from the "Dreamtime".

Language — The dispersion of the native populations across the Australian continent led to a significant diversity of spoken languages. At the time of colonisation, more than two hundred were recorded for a population estimated at one million individuals. For the Aborigines, language is a fundamental element of their identity but does not play a role in their political structure.

Dreamtime — This is a translation by the ethnologist Karel Kupka of the concept of "Dreamtime", which is itself a transposition by the anthropologists Spencer and Gillen of the term *Altyerrenge*, used by the Arrernte people to define the origins of the universe. The "Dreamtime" represents the mythical time of the creation of the world. It is also referred to as the "ancestral past" because it constitutes the "era of the Ancestors". Thus, it provides the essential backdrop to the cosmology of all the indigenous groups in Australia. While accounts vary, adapt, and differ depending on the context within which the linguistic groups, clans, and social groups evolve, they all retain a single central structure: the time of the creation of the Ancestors who, through their wanderings, gave birth to the universe in all its diversity and founded the rites and beliefs that were transmitted through a specific initiation process for both men and women.

Tjukurrpa — The Warlpiri use this word to define the Ancestors, spiritual and mythical beings who predate human existence, which they helped to create. In the course of their peregrinations, the Ancestors created nature in such a way that man would come to inhabit it, bearing the responsibility of ensuring its sustainability. These Ancestors come in all forms — human or animal, vegetable or mineral — and can freely change their state. Although they belong to the "Dreamtime", the ancestors remain present beyond this mythical period. As the source of all spiritual power and guardians of world order through rituals and ceremonies, they exert an influence on the world. Additionally, the participation of these spirits in the creation of the individual secures a continuous link between the present and the "Dreamtime".

JOHNNY WARANGKULA TJUPURRULA

Johnny Warangkula Tjupurrula (ca. 1918–2001) was the first Papunya Tula artist to create "totemic landscapes" with a naturalistic flair closely resembling the Western concept of landscape. He also pioneered the use of the dotting technique as an analogy for desert vegetation. His work fully reflects this aesthetic, while also providing an autobiographical narrative that rekindles memories of transhumance through the Western Desert.

In 1923, in an effort to protect the cattle, the government issued the Dingo Destruction Ordinance, whereby it agreed to pay for the scalps of slaughtered dingoes. This ordinance became one of the few sources of income for Aboriginal hunters. By the mid-1940s, the bounty rose to one pound per kill. Just like Charlie Tarawa Tjungurrayi (see pp. 14–16) and Nosepeg Tjupurrula, Johnny Warangkula Tjupurrula left his family at Haasts Bluff settlement to head west in a small camel caravan. While tracking dingoes, the hunters explored traditional sites that had been abandoned. *Dingo Camp at Tinki* recounts this rarely documented episode (only six paintings from 1973 are related to this theme), and is a throwback to ancient times, in the midst of the ancestral practices of the Pintupi, a world away from colonial standards.

Parallel running sand dunes, vast salt lakes, and bushy plains shape the Pintupi landscape. The artist depicts the caves, rocky outcrops, and crevices where dingoes make their dens. Johnny Warangkula Tjupurrula's painting is in keeping with a lineage of songs recounting the epic of the Dingoes. His melodic sense of informality was fed by these sung tales referring to the Dingo Ancestor. On the canvas, an adult dingo brings back the meat its puppies have been waiting for back to its den. The puppies have left their footprints along the tracks laid down by the eldest. The den is marked by concentric circles devoid of any decoration. The bare ground unfolds like a vast unpainted landscape.

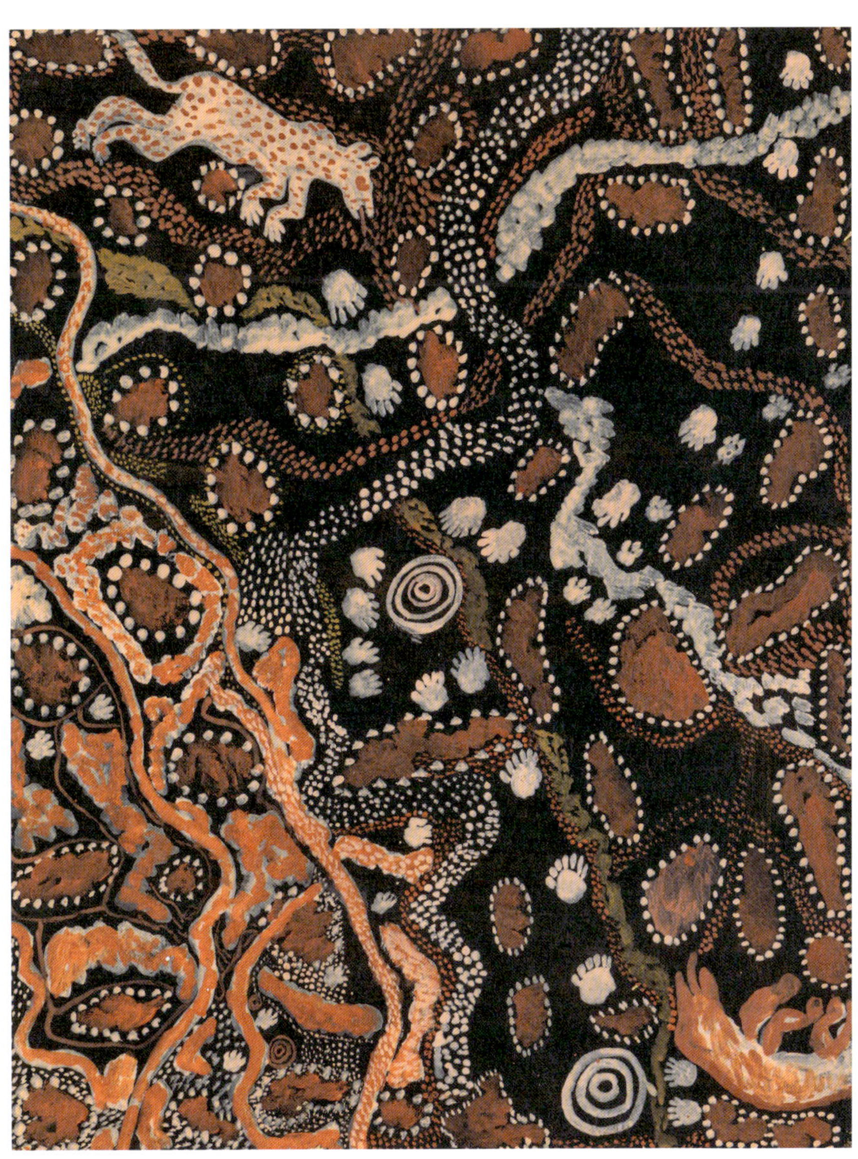

Dingo Camp at Tinki, 1973

Acrylic on canvas, 79 × 61 cm
Philippson Collection

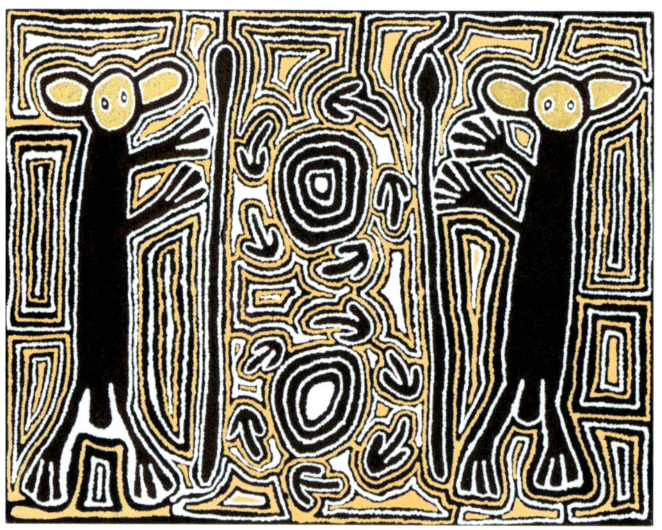

Linda Syddick Napaltjarri – *Kangoroo Man Story*, 2014
Acrylic on canvas, 78 × 103 cm, Philippson Collection

The early days of contemporary Aboriginal painting in Papunya Tula

In November 1973, Peter Fanin gave each of the ten artists in the Papunya Tula cooperative two boards of the same size: 122 by 92 centimetres. The men, who had varying degrees of skill, gathered in the Panunya Tula "workshop" and engaged in lengthy discussions about the appropriateness of painting their sacred stories on wooden boards. Kaapa Tjampitjinpa played an important role in the decision. The disclosure of initiation knowledge hitherto reserved exclusively for strictly supervised and codified ceremonies raised many questions and concerns. A number of spiritual leaders issued warnings to those who wanted to give free rein to their imagination, and Kaapa was threatened more than once: "Your children and my children will die as a result of the things revealed in the paintings." Painting truths that had been passed on orally or during rituals was a subject of bitter discussion. At the end of these talks, however, it was finally agreed to pursue the project.

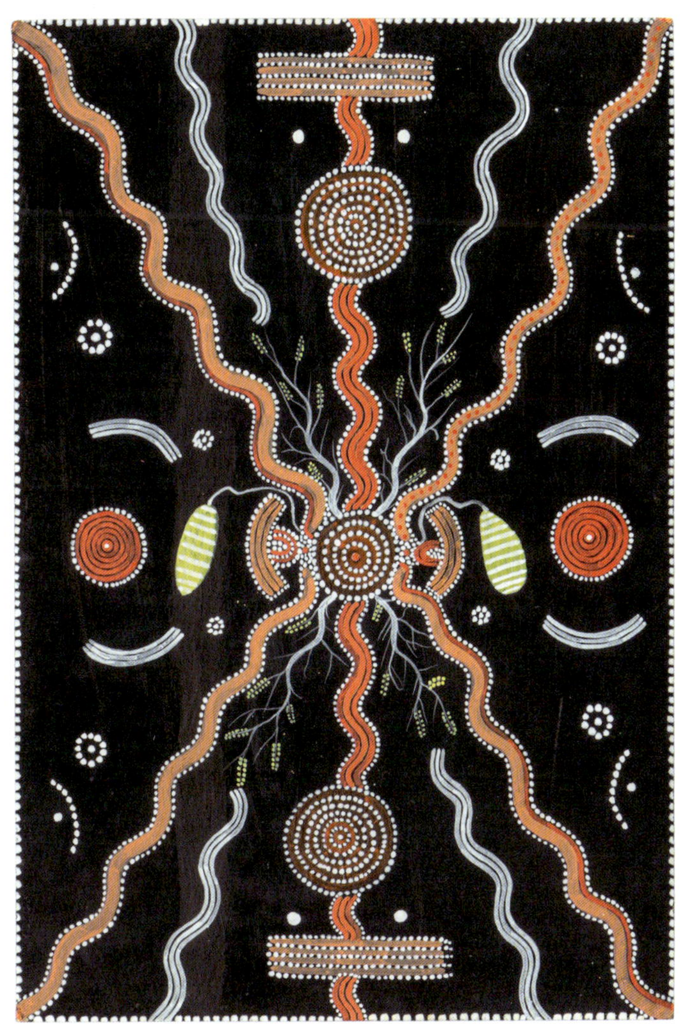

Yala at Yantjupu, 1973

Acrylic on canvas, 55 × 37 cm
Philippson Collection

CHARLIE TAWARA TJUNGURRAYI

Born in the west of Kintore, Charlie Tawara Tjungurrayi (ca. 1921–1999) belonged to the Pintupi tribe. In the 1930s, he was one of the first members of his community to migrate eastwards. Settling at the Christian mission in Hermannsburg where he became friends with Charlie Tjararu, he worked on army construction sites. This was his first exposure to Western culture and his first contact with the "Whitefellas" from Europe, whom the Aborigines distrusted to the extent that they would take their children out of school. In the early 1950s, Charlie Tawara Tjungurrayi settled in Haasts Bluff with his family while exploring the Western Desert.

As a Pintupi, he was one of the group of men who started painting in 1971 upon Geoffrey Bardon's invitation. The name Papunya Tula, which means "a meeting place for all brothers and cousins", was coined by him. However, this adventure was primarily driven by financial considerations: Charlie Tawara Tjungurrayi believed that the commercialisation of these ethnic artefacts would help improve the financial situation of the community at Papunya Tula. He was one of the people who considered returning to his home territory to set up shop there. With his energy and determination and his knowledge of English, he helped clarify the Pintupi discourse within the group and asserted himself as the spokesman for the Aboriginal painters. This earned him the

Willy Tjungurrayi
Untitled – Tali Tjuta, 2004

Acrylic on Belgian linen, 111 × 102 cm
Philippson Collection

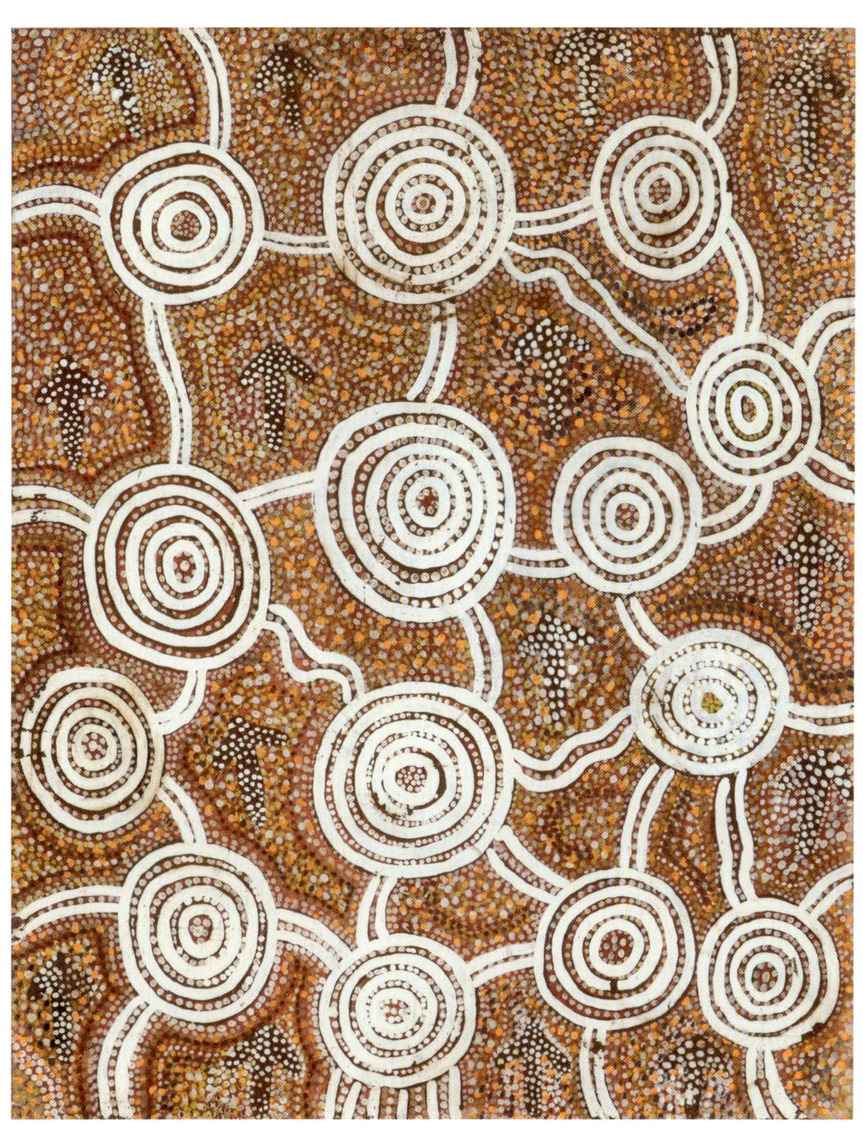

Untitled (Emu Dreaming), 1975

Acrylic on canvas, 76 × 60 cm
Philippson Collection

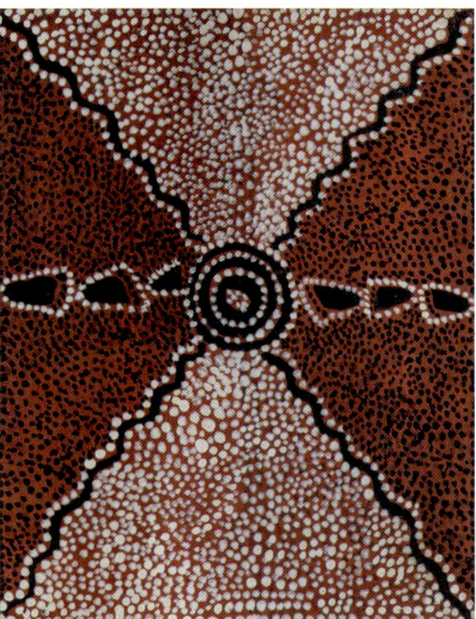

Shorty Lungkarta Tjungurrayi
Death Story, 1972
Acrylic on canvas, 36 × 23 cm
Philippson Collection

reputation of being "devious", "bitter" or "difficult" in the eyes of some Western administrators. In contrast, Geoffrey Bardon praised his open-mindedness and capacity for openness, which made him a mediator between two cultures that had previously ignored each other. Charlie Tawara Tjungurrayi's skill lay in overcoming the paradox inherent in an artistic activity that was perceived as new, while at the same time perpetuating an age-old tradition whose ritualistic foundations would be transformed into an economic activity. As a member of the Tjungurrayi group (Kingsley, Shorty Lungkarta [see here below], Yala Yala and Don [see on right page], George, Willy [see p. 14], Two Bob and Yumpululu), Charlie Tawara acted as the "leader" and as such, he took care of the community's interests while simultaneously emerging as a prolific painter.

The controversy over what could be shown and what was forbidden gave Charlie Tawara the opportunity to demonstrate his sense of compromise. To resolve a crisis that threatened the integrity of the group, Bardon suggested depicting everyday activities, such as those conveyed in children's stories — the gathering of food, for example. Charlie Tawara echoed this view with his 1972 *Ya Dreaming*, a painting on cardboard intended to teach young children where and how to find food in the desert.

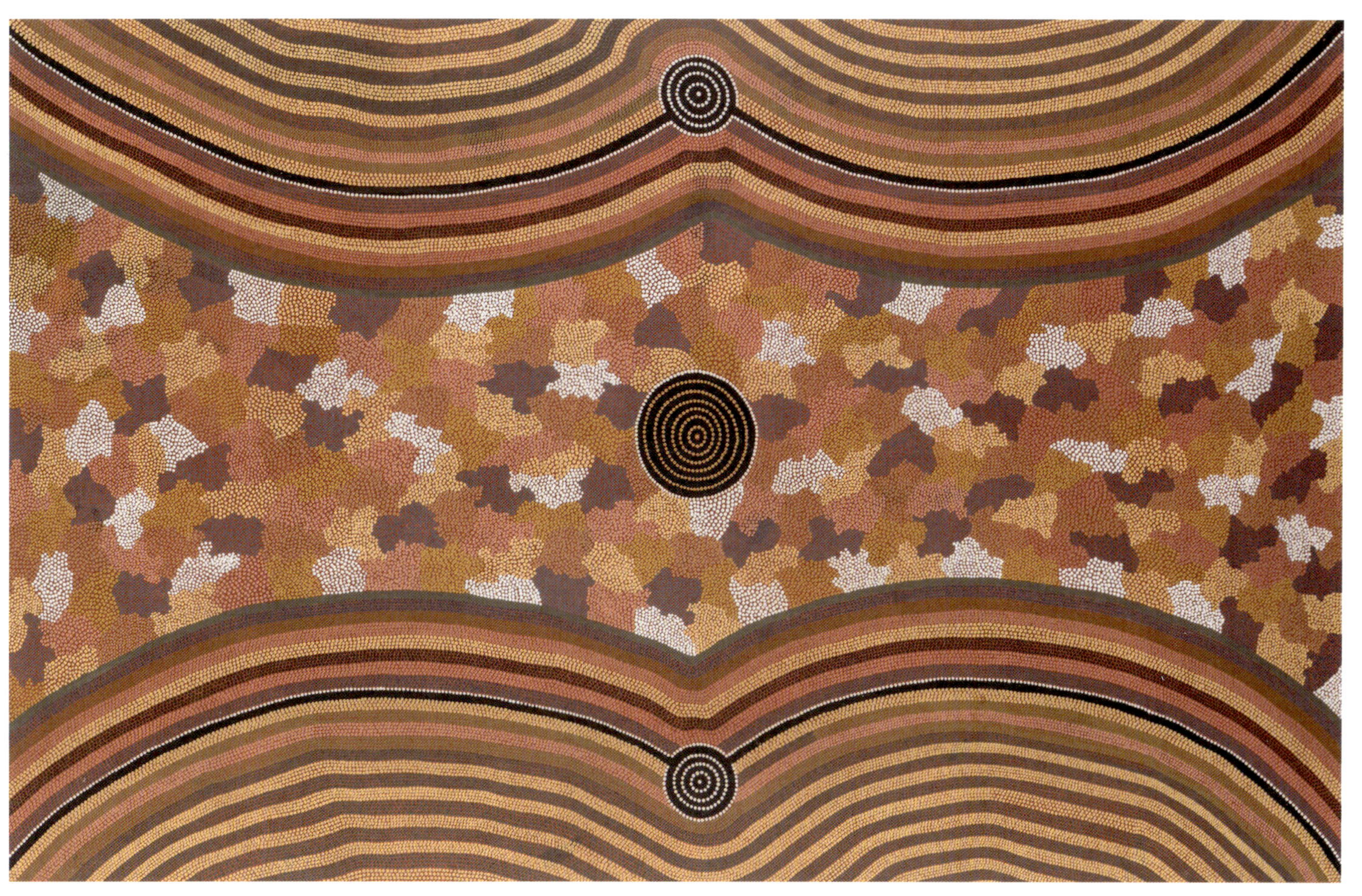

Men's Corroboree, 1993

Acrylic on linen, 118 × 190 cm
Philippson Collection

GEORGE TJUNGURRAYI

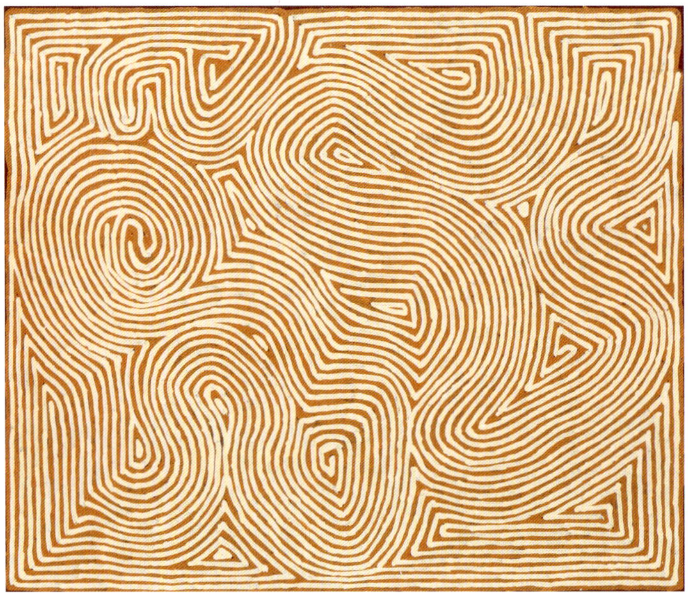

Mamultjulkunga, 2004
Acrylic on canvas, 76 × 91 cm, Philippson Collection

Born in the bush in the area around Kiwirrkurra (Western Australia), George Tjungurrayi (ca. 1947) started painting in 1976. His work attempts to depict the Tingari cycles associated with the sacred lands and sites traversed by the great Ancestors of this ethnic group. The artist evokes the clay deposits of Mamultjukunga, a soggy spot northwest of Lake McKay, where his father died. According to Aboriginal mythology, two Ancestors — one from the Tjangala family, the other from the Tjapaltjarri sub-section — set up camp in this area. After a rain shower, the clay pit turned into a cool lake. A full-bodied plant that usually grows under the shrubs (*Tecticornia verrucosa*) thrived in the area. Its seeds are gathered and ground into dough that the Tjangala and Tjapaltjarri people have kneaded and baked ever since the ancestral event to which their families were linked.

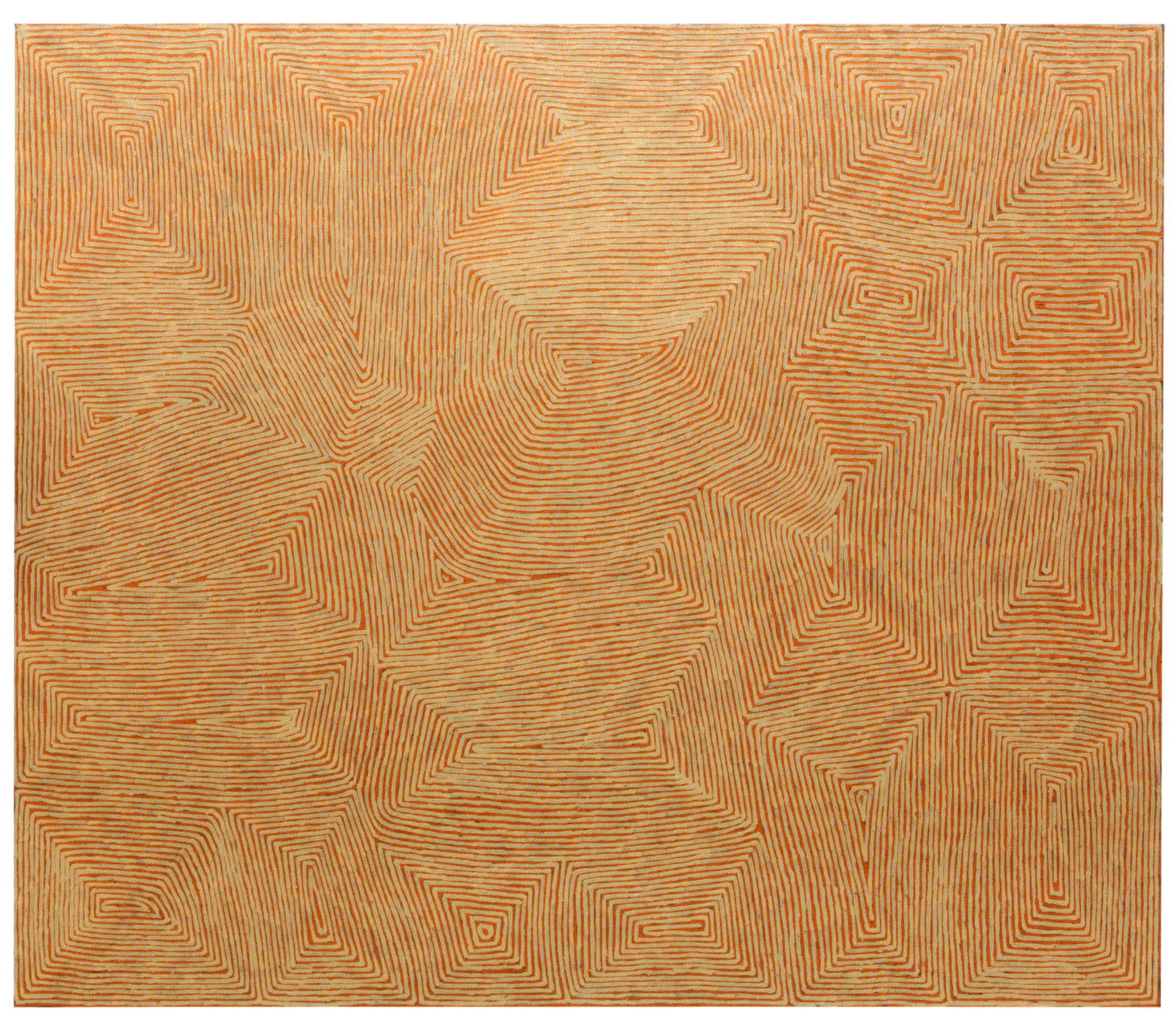

Mamultjulkunga, 2013

Acrylic on canvas, 152 × 182 cm
Philippson Collection

A prominent figure in Aboriginal art, Clifford Possum Tjapaltjarri (ca. 1932–2002) was the son of Gwoya Jungarai, better known as "One Pound Jimmy", who embodied the quintessential Aborigine in the eyes of Australians since the publication of his photographic portrait by Roy Dunstan in *Walkabout* magazine. A member of the Anmatyerre people, Clifford Possum started painting in the 1960s with Kaapa Tjampitjinpa and his brother Tim Leura Tjapaltjarri. He was one of the leading figures of the first generation of artists who were brought together in Papunya Tula. His work gained a stellar reputation. He was the first Aboriginal artist to win the Alice Prize with a painting entitled *Mulga Seed Dreaming*. His sense of colour and composition, the sharpness of his brushwork, and the amplitude of the narratives he embraced had considerable influence on the development of the first generation of Aboriginal painters, keen to transpose their initiatory traditions into representations based on the Western model. For Clifford Possum Tjapaltjarri, the key to promoting Aboriginal culture was to make it visible and understandable to the dominant culture. To this end, the artist must appropriate the very forms of the

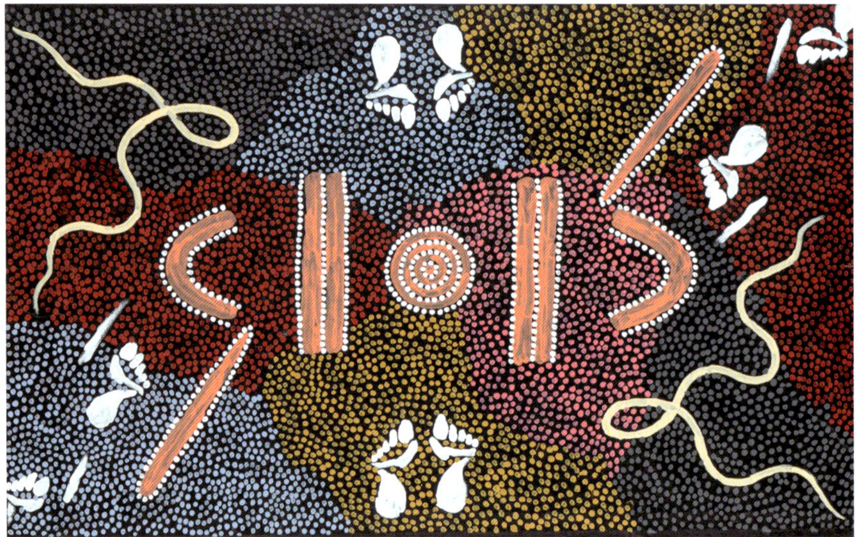

Untitled, 2001
Acrylic on canvas, 92 × 151 cm, Philippson Collection

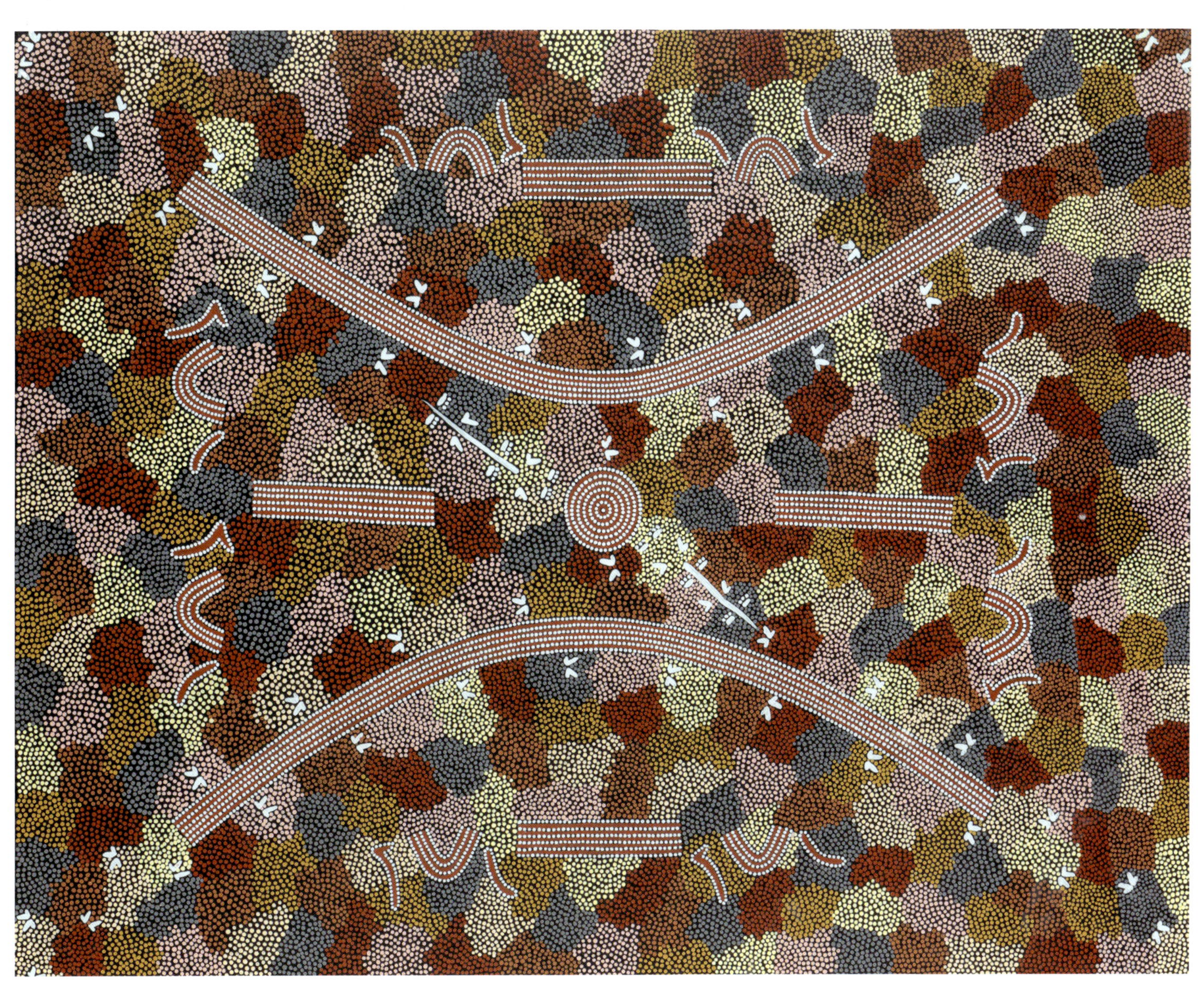

Rock Wallaby Dreaming, 1986

Acrylic on canvas, 127 × 162 cm
Philippson Collection

21

"other's" narrative in order to clarify a hitherto invisible Aboriginal heritage. The acknowledgement of the market itself will thus constitute the expression of an awareness of the Aboriginal identity. And this, without the secret meaning of the "Dreamtime" being completely explored, since the understanding of the representation is based on the description — as incomplete as it is subjective — that is given.

In *Untitled (Honey Ant Dreaming*, see p. 20*)*, a piece that typifies Clifford Possum Tjapaltjarri's rich and precise style, the artist focuses on the symbolic patterns traced on the ground during the ritual associated with the "Honey Ant Dreaming" (*Yurampi Tjukurrpa*), a ceremony that takes place on Yuelamu Mountain, northwest of Alice Springs. The concentric circles in the middle of the composition represent the water hole that determined the destination of the place during "Dreamtime". As the Honey Ant was coming into being, a group set up camp here, making the site very important for the performance of initiation rituals. The horizontal U-shaped configurations represent men holding the digging stick by their side. In front of them, they have placed the decorated eucalyptus planks recounting the story of the Honey Ant. At the top and bottom, footprints are depicted on the ground, which is made up of several dotted areas. In Clifford Possum Tjapaltjarri's view, this colourful patchwork reflects the changing nature of the desert at different times and seasons.

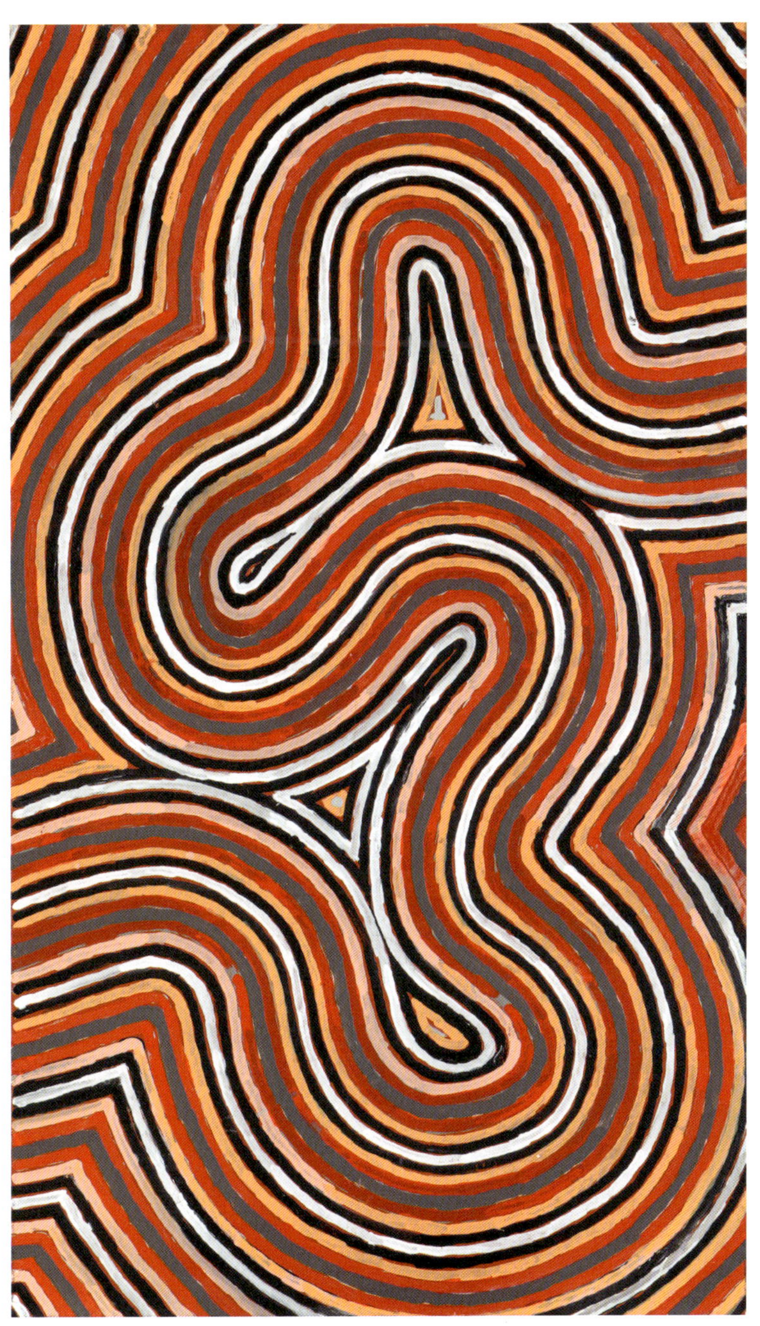

Walk Around Worm at Napperby, 1995

Acrylic on canvas, 125 × 75 cm
Philippson Collection

GABRIELLA POSSUM NUNGURRAYI

Born in the Central Desert region, Gabriella Possum Nungarrayi (ca. 1967) is the eldest daughter of Clifford Possum Tjapaltjarri. However, this patriarchal and very Western genealogy is not prevalent in Aboriginal communities in the same form. Gabriella speaks the Anmatyerre language.

As winner of the Alice Springs Art Prize in 1983, Gabriella Possum Nungarrayi has received widespread praise for a body of work described as "innovative" and "culturally significant". Her work is at once modern and contemporary, while remaining true to her Aboriginal heritage and the affirmation of an identity to which her father and grandfather contributed. Her work reflects this double inclination towards cultural integration and the search for innovation.

The painting *Grand Mother Country* depicts the Gold Country bush, her grandmother's homeland near Mount Allan in the Northern Territory. While her father and grandfather are well known to us, we know nothing of her grandmother's activities, or whether she belongs to her paternal or maternal bloodline. The strange landscape abounds with activity that escapes any interpretation based solely on the transcription of the visible into the legible. It is a vast sandy expanse studded with forests and shrubbery, where the artist spent part of her childhood at her grandmother's side. Seated women are symbolised by light-coloured "U"s; they wear body paint and sing, surrounded by brightly coloured cockatoo feathers. The ritual action they are engaged in aims to ensure the continued existence of plant and animal life in an ancestral setting.

As a woman painter, Gabriella Possum Nungurrayi thus depicts a female ritual from which men are excluded by transposing the emblems of these initiation rites and some of their forms, which are directly invoked on the canvas. We can sense the tension of the painted bodies, embellished with cockatoo

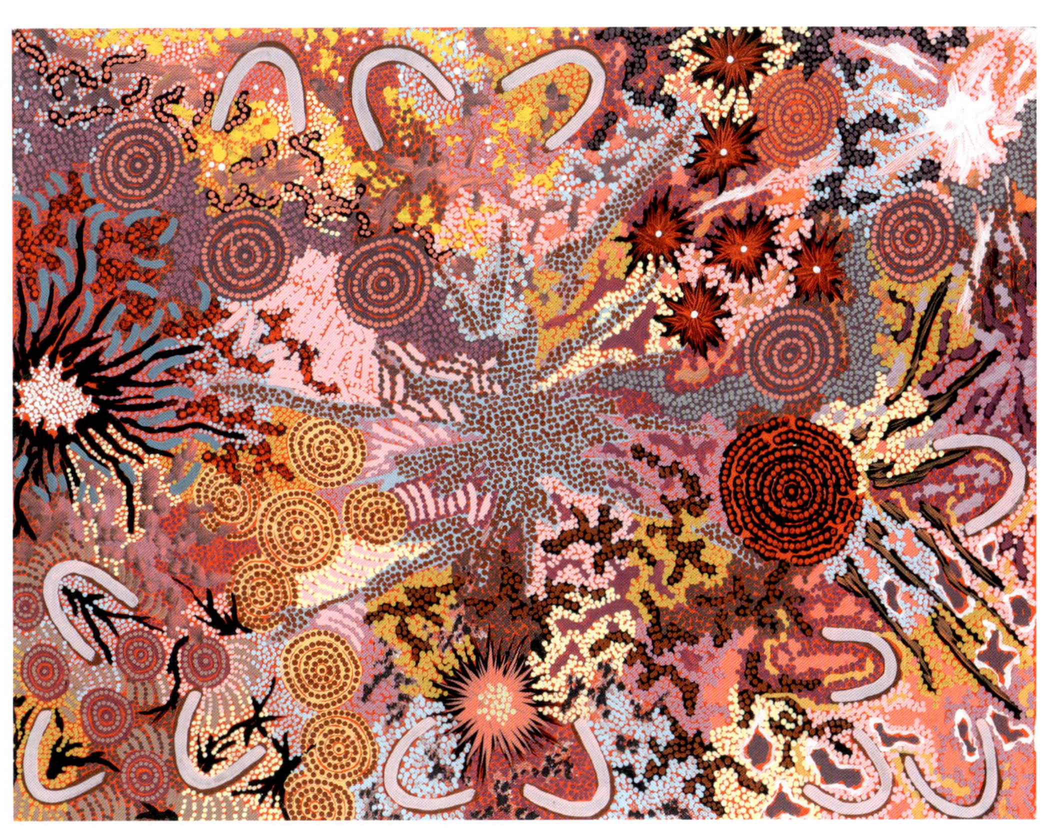

Grand Mother Country, 2015

Acrylic on canvas, 80 × 100 cm
Philippson Collection

feathers, moving through space to the sound of repetitive chants; we can glimpse the wild flowers and plants that, like *spinifex*, sprinkle the ground with warm colours. The colours and shapes refer to the wealth of food in the bush and to its healing remedies, used since the dawn of time. This abundance works in cycles to sustain life. The lines depict ancestral toponymies through which the genesis of the country is narrated: water holes, rocks. In short, the history of the Aboriginal people through its landscape. The whole is perceived from such a height that the representation is reconstructed like an aerial view. As though the viewpoint was at high altitude and the painting had been transformed into the map of a dream unfolding in colour and sound.

The subject of the piece goes far beyond the action "represented", however symbolically. Joyous and generous, the painting celebrates the fertility of the country by drawing from a ritual that, repeated on a specific date, creates the conditions for this immemorial continuity. In another predominantly blue version, Gabriella Possum Nungarrayi depicts the conditions of happiness as perceived by the Aborigines: a state of symbiosis with the landscape which, through rituals, keeps the spirit of the Ancestors alive, guaranteeing the vitality and fertility of the region. From this permanence, she deducts the social role of women as guardians of the "bush tucker", as the vestals of fertility, requiring ceremony, body painting, and invocation of the Ancestors through song and dance. This social function does not stem from a negotiated "social contract" as the proponents of globalised postmodernity would like to believe. It is the result of progressive change, made from endless returns to the past: to that moment which the "Dreamtime" has been repeating tirelessly since the dawn of time.

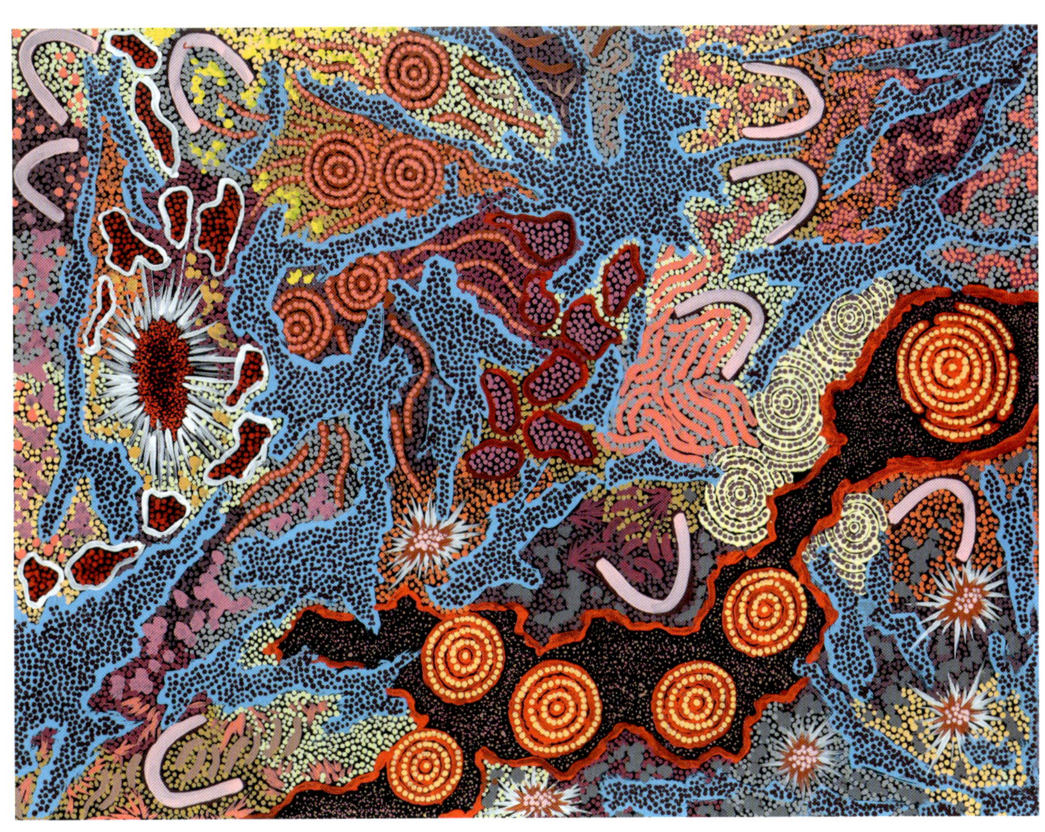

My Country

Acrylic on canvas, 80 × 100 cm
Philippson Collection

Siblings Thomas (ca. 1964) and Walala (ca. 1972) Tjapaltjarri are Pintupi artists. Before coming of age, they lived with their family in the Wilkinkarra region without ever coming into contact with Westerners. As part of a group of nine individuals (the *Pintupi Nine*), they roamed the Gibson Desert re-enacting the 50,000-year old lifestyle of hunter-gatherers, living naked and only armed with spears and boomerangs. In 1984, the group moved to Kiwirrkurra in the traditional Pintupi territory that had been returned to the group at the beginning of the 80s in the context of the Aboriginal Land Rights movement. There, they were reunited with several family members, some of whom they had been apart from for more than two decades. Walala and his brother Thomas were educated there and took part in a renaissance of aboriginal spirituality, which is now closely linked to the development of painting using the principles initiated in Papunya Tula in 1973.

As relatives of Warlimpirrnga Tjapaltjarri (see pp. 32–33), the two brothers started painting in 1987. From the outset, they depicted Tingari "dreams" that had occurred on the route connecting the sacred sites of Marruwa, Kakarrara, and Wilurrara. These mythical tales, common to all the tribes living in the desert, reveal essential initiatory knowledge.

The Tingari Ancestors — according to tradition, a group of men followed by a group of women and a third group of so-called novices — embarked on endless peregrinations that took them from the sea to the heart of the Australian desert. These journeys also took them across the salt marshes of central Australia, where they enjoyed adventures that feed directly into both male and female rituals. The two brothers address this landscape with their tightly woven patterns.

The symbols used in Thomas' painting are borrowed from the traditional repertoire as seen in rock carvings or in the ornamentation of shields, thrusters, or boomerangs. Here, the depiction is closely linked to the many sandhills (*tali tjuta*) of the Marruwa region, west of Lake McKay. The painter has specifically linked the space of his painting to the site of Wanapatangu where

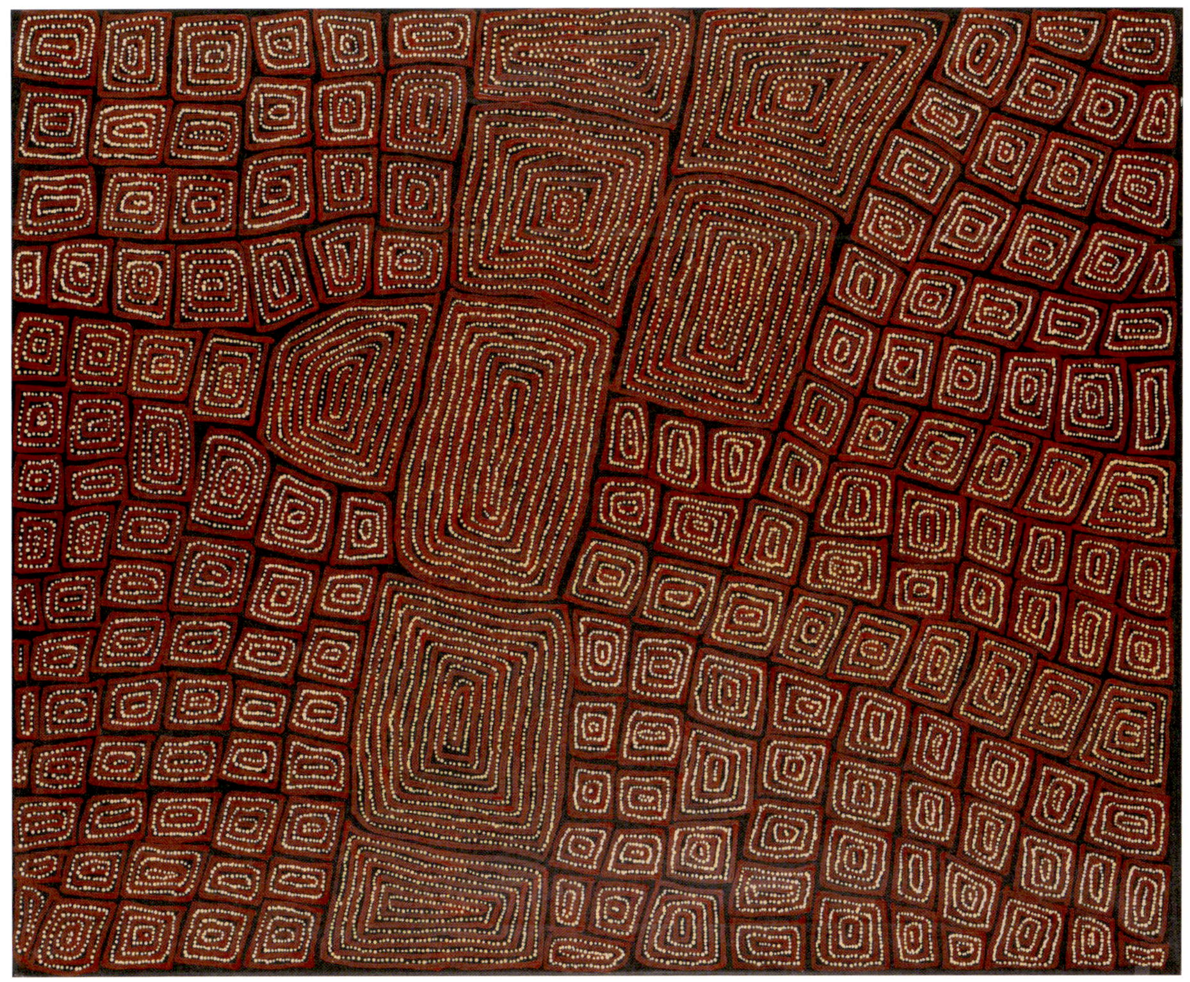

Thomas Tjapaltjarri – *Tingari*, 2010

Acrylic on canvas, 122 × 152 cm
Philippson Collection

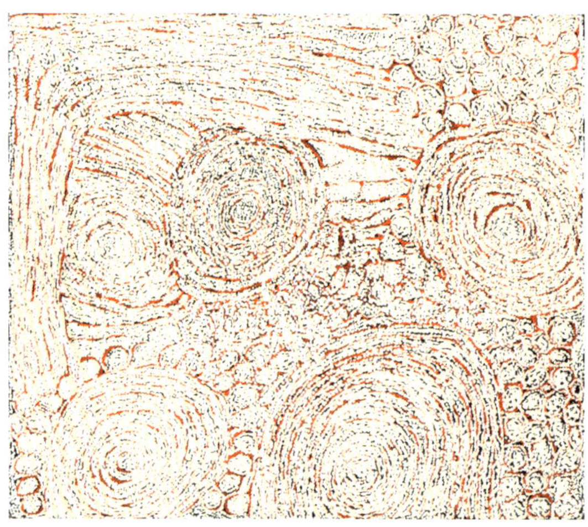

Walangkura Tjapaltjarri – *Untitled*
Acrylic on canvas, 91 × 122 cm, Philippson Collection

the Tingari Ancestors held a ceremony that is still alive in the male community. Thomas preserves the traditional formulation of the pattern as it appears in rock carvings or body paintings.

Walala (also known as Robert Yattjatjazzinya) provides a more contemporary, abstract interpretation. Through his intertwined pattern, the tortuous paths walked by his Ancestors emerge, as they created the first rites and laid the foundations of life in society. Anthropologists consider the Tingari epic as the ultimate poetic recollection of the last migration from Asia some 6,000 years ago.

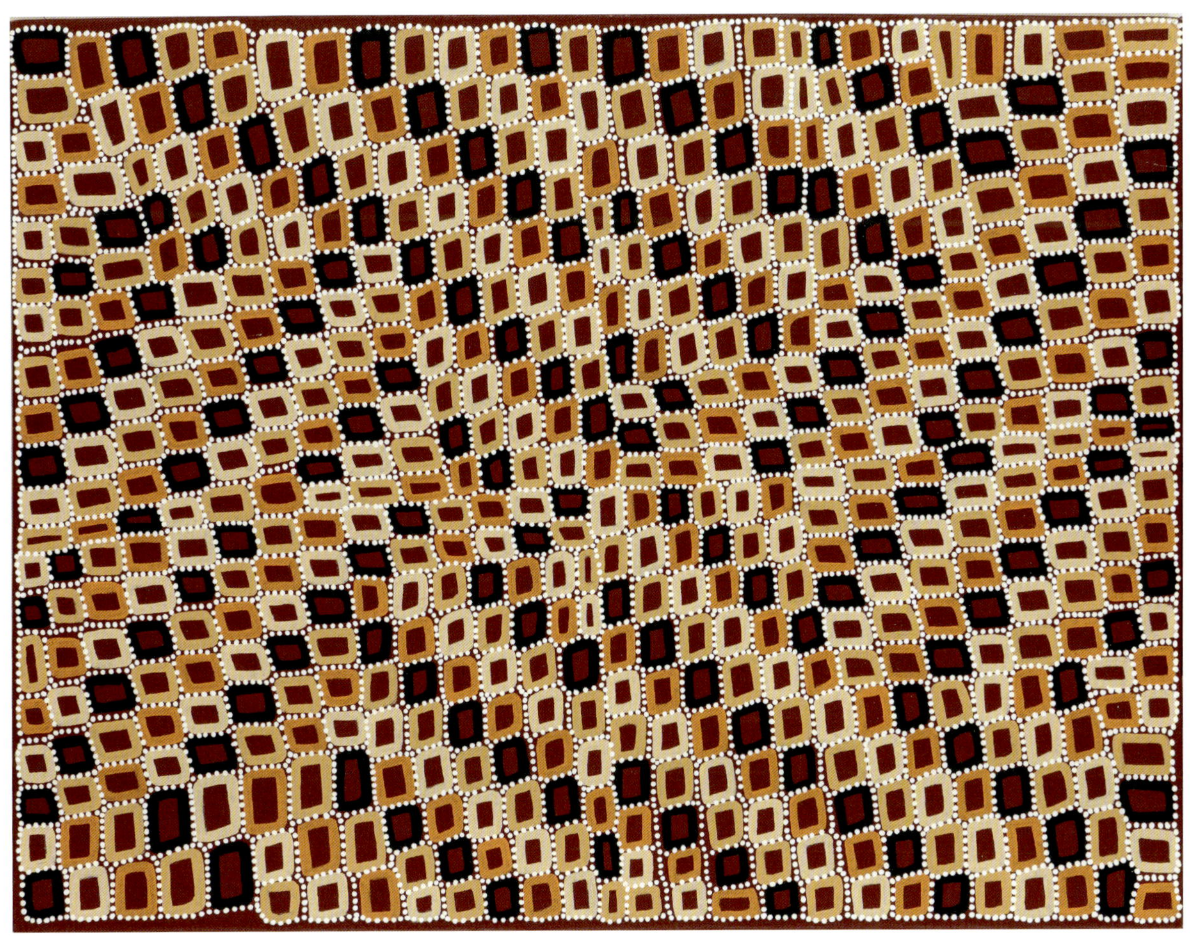

Walala Tjapaltjarri – *Tingari*, 2014

Acrylic on canvas, 122 × 152 cm
Philippson Collection

WARLIMPIRRNGA TJAPALTJARRI

Warlimpirrnga Tjapaltjarri is a member of the renowned "Pintupi Nine". Born around 1959, he is from a community that had no contact with Western civilisation until 1984, when they were displaced to Kiwirrkura. There he began to paint at the community centre, joining the older Pintupi artists who had lived in Papunya Tula since 1971. His work corresponds to the norms of Western Desert painting, as elaborated in Papunya Tula: dot work, symbolic formal codes referring to the "Dreamtime", an initiatory dimension and the upholding of ancestral traditions. In 2015, marked visual development is apparent: his latest paintings have only retained a basic outline from traditional practice, evoking the patterns emblazoned on shields. The dot has become a line to convey vital energy in an undulating movement. The traditional motif evokes sand dunes (*tali tjuta*) and clay deposits (*kapi*).

Warlimpirrnga Tjapaltjarri particularly focuses on the vast swamp, Minatapinya, where the Tingara people set up camp during their mythical wanderings. The area is known for its Water Snake Ancestors. In the artist's own words, the network of wavy lines designates the watery areas around Lake McKay.

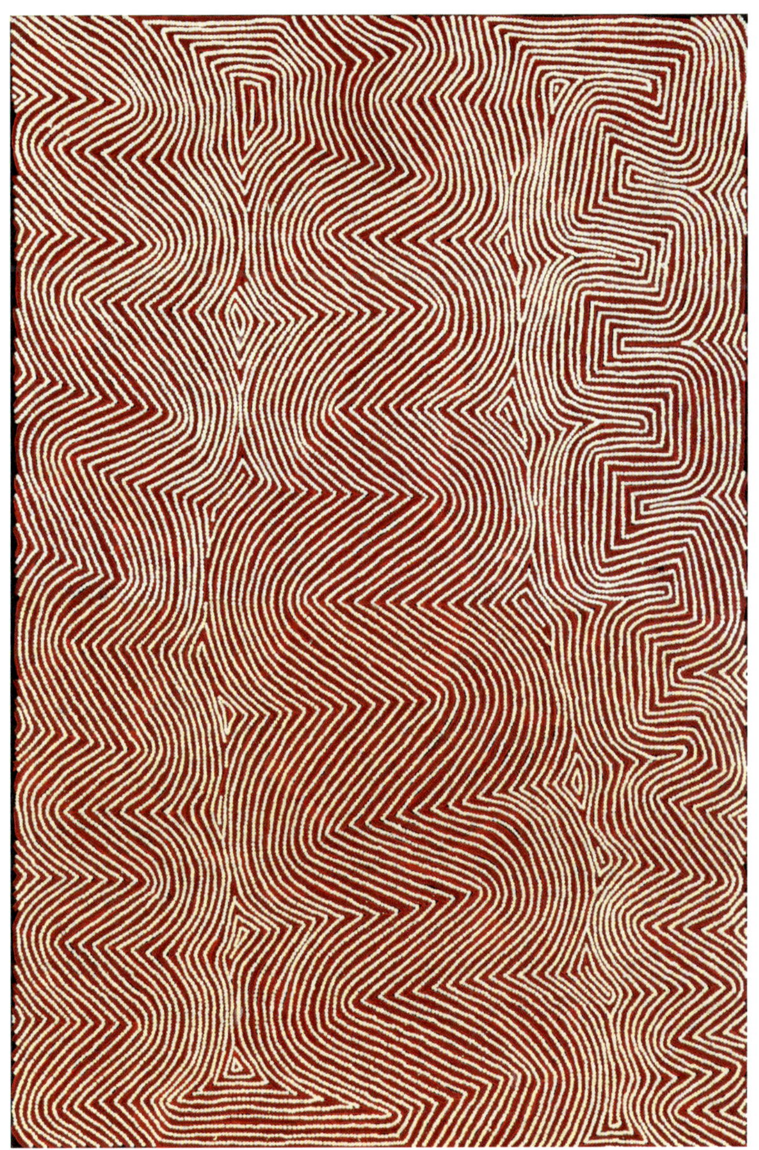

Tingari, 2015

Acrylic on paper, 91 × 122 cm
Philippson Collection

CHARLIE TJAPANGATI

Charlie Tjapangati (ca. 1949) was born in Palinpalintjanya, northwest of Juniper Well. In 1964, after receiving a full induction to traditional teachings, he went to Papunya with his family. There, he helped build the settlement in exchange for food. In 1978, having observed the elders, he started painting pictures that would quickly earn him recognition in the art world. In 1982, Charlie Tjapangati changed residence and moved with other Pintupi to the Kintore settlement. From his beginnings, the artist has depicted the stories related to the ceremonies of the Tingari cycle. The narrative elements that shape the "Dream" are simply one level of understanding. A piece like this cannot be regarded simply as the recounting of a mythical episode. The Aboriginal imagination is imbued with deep cultural references that transcend narrative logic and its "simple" interpretation in a Western spectator's sense. The spiritual resonance of the portrayal addresses the very foundations of the identity of each individual, in its filial — matri- or patrilineal — relationships, as well as totemic relationships or in the spiritual elements linked to each site. Accessing the different layers of cosmological meaning requires the completion of the various stages of initiation and cannot be understood at a glance.

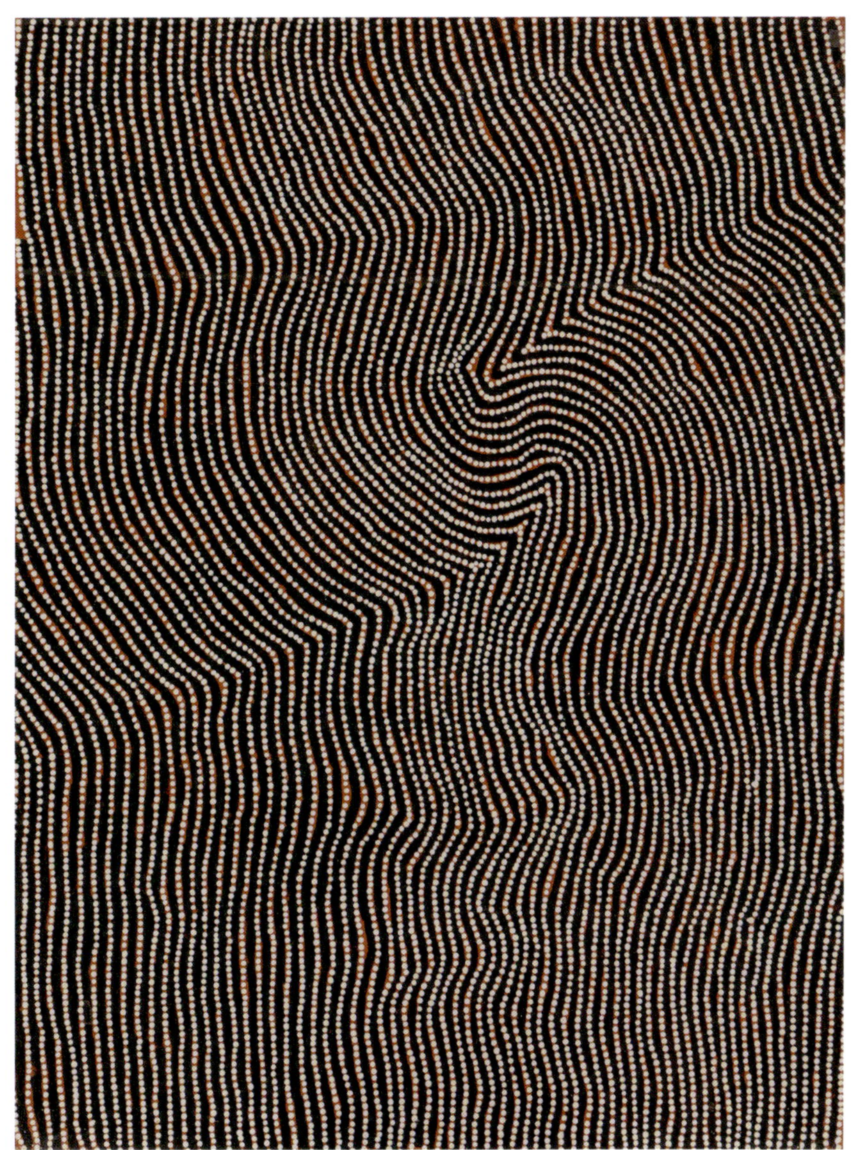

Tingari Cycle

Acrylic on canvas, 122 × 92 cm
Philippson Collection

TJAWINA PORTER NAMPITJINPA

Tjawina Porter Nampitjinpa was born around 1950 on the north side of the Docker River in Western Australia. Half-sister to Nyurapayia Nampitjinpa, she grew up in the bush with her family before moving to Papunya. Later, she moved back to her homeland. Renowned for her skills as a traditional basket weaver and for her paintings, she illustrates the dreams of her father and mother through the sites of Yumari, Punkilpirri, Tjukurla, and Tjalili, locations that are central for their springs and food supplies, and celebrated during important ceremonies. *Punkilpirri* evokes the activities associated with the site of Punkilpirri, one of the many waterholes near Tjawina's place of origin on the edge of the Northern Territory. The symbols also refer to bush foods, such as bush tomatoes (*kampurarpara*), which are prepared during rituals. There is also a digging stick (*wana*) painted in dark ochre that is used to find food. These intricately adorned sticks play a central role in rituals where they are used as clapping sticks.

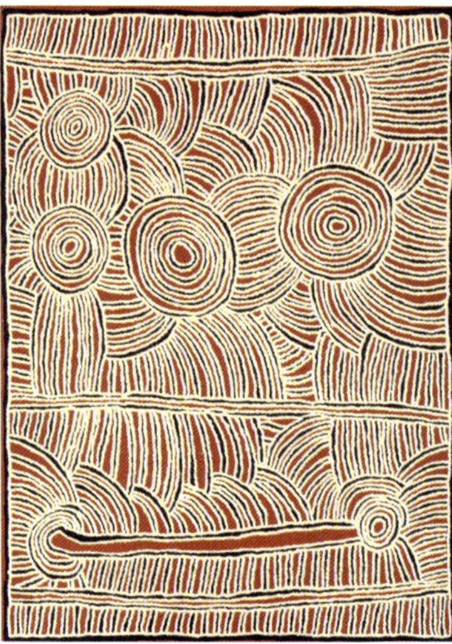

Punkilpirri, 2009

Acrylic on canvas, 122 × 91 cm
Philippson Collection

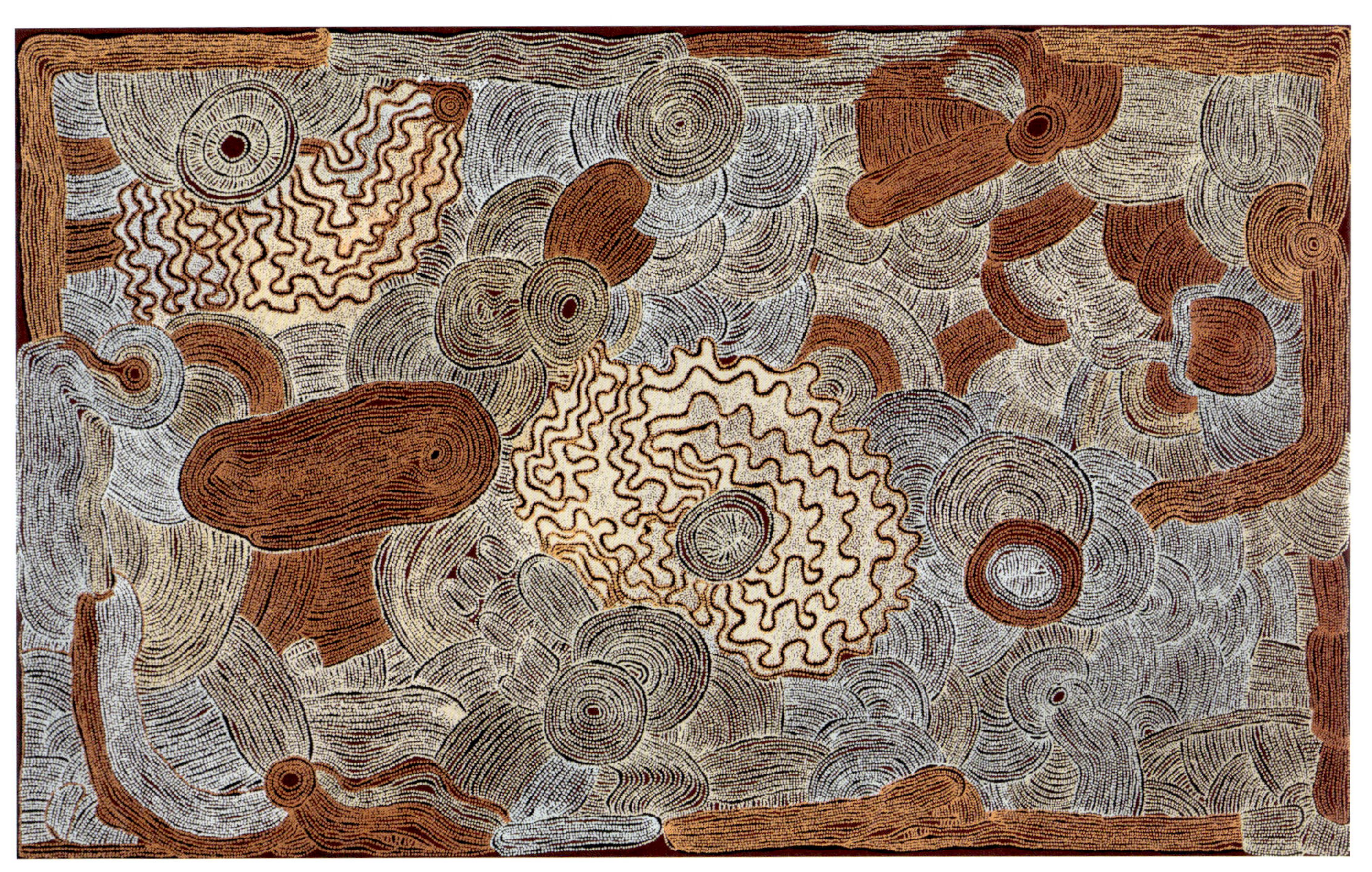

Tjalili, 2009

Acrylic on linen, 181 × 305 cm
RMFAB, donated by Yanda Aboriginal Art, Alice Springs (Australia), 2020, inv. 12599

MAISIE CAMPBELL NAPALTJARRI

Born near Haasts Bluff, also referred to as Ikuntji, Maisie Campbell Napaltjarri (ca. 1958) grew up in Papunya Tula, where she went to school before moving to Kintore on the borders of Western Australia and the Northern Territory. She started painting in the early 1990s. Her motifs evoke the sites associated with women's ceremonies (*minyma inmaku*). The sacred rocks in the Kintore area are a major site for Pintupi ceremonies and Maisie Campbell represents them while displaying traditional forms associated with the stories she has documented there.

The piece *Kapi Tjukurrpa, Minyma Inmaku* (2011) depicts the "Dream of Water", (*kapi tjukurrpa* in the Pintupi language). In this work, the artist shows us the sites associated with her ancestral territories. In this landscape, the spirit of the serpent Liru and his ancestral warrior people are slumbering. The concentric shapes evoke important places of ceremony, showing — amongst other things — the sand hill country (*tali*), the rocky outcrops (*puli*), and the freshwater springs essential to the populations of the Western Desert. It is thought that Maisie's mother drank this water when she was pregnant. The artist's identity is thus linked to the site, and for this reason, Maisie Campbell reproduces her spiritual birthplace in her own manner. She evokes both the physical characteristics of the land and the conditions of its creation and ceremonial songs. Set between the Northern Territory and Western Australia, Pancoedi is an arid, deep-red rock site set in a fault line in the middle of the rocky hills. Transparent waterfalls have created two lakes there.

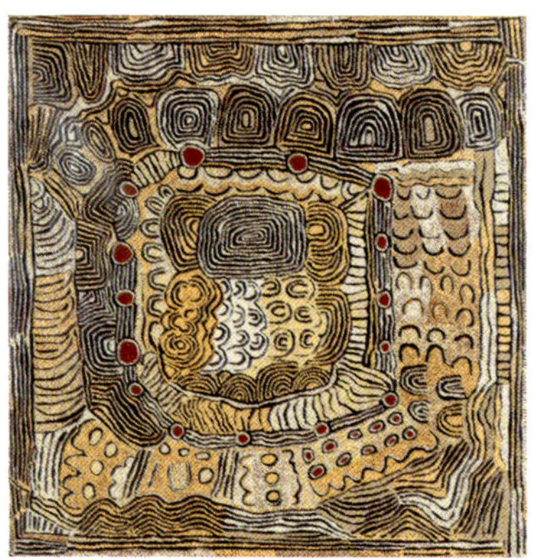

Kapi Tjukurrpa & Women Ceremonies, 2011

Acrylic on canvas, 152 × 152 cm
Philippson Collection

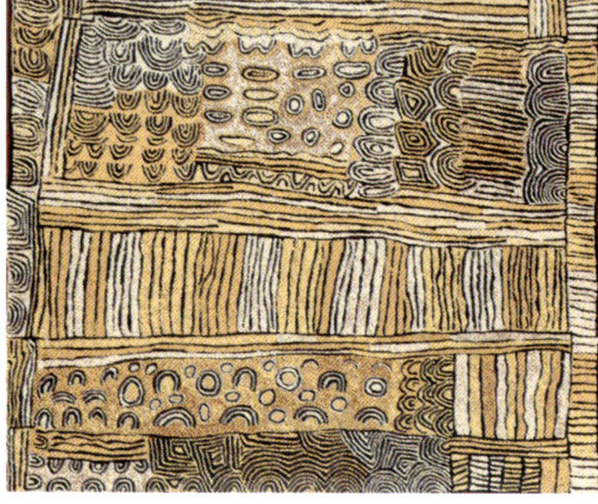

Kapi Tjukurrpa, Minyma Inmaku, 2011

Acrylic on canvas, 152 × 183 cm
Philippson Collection

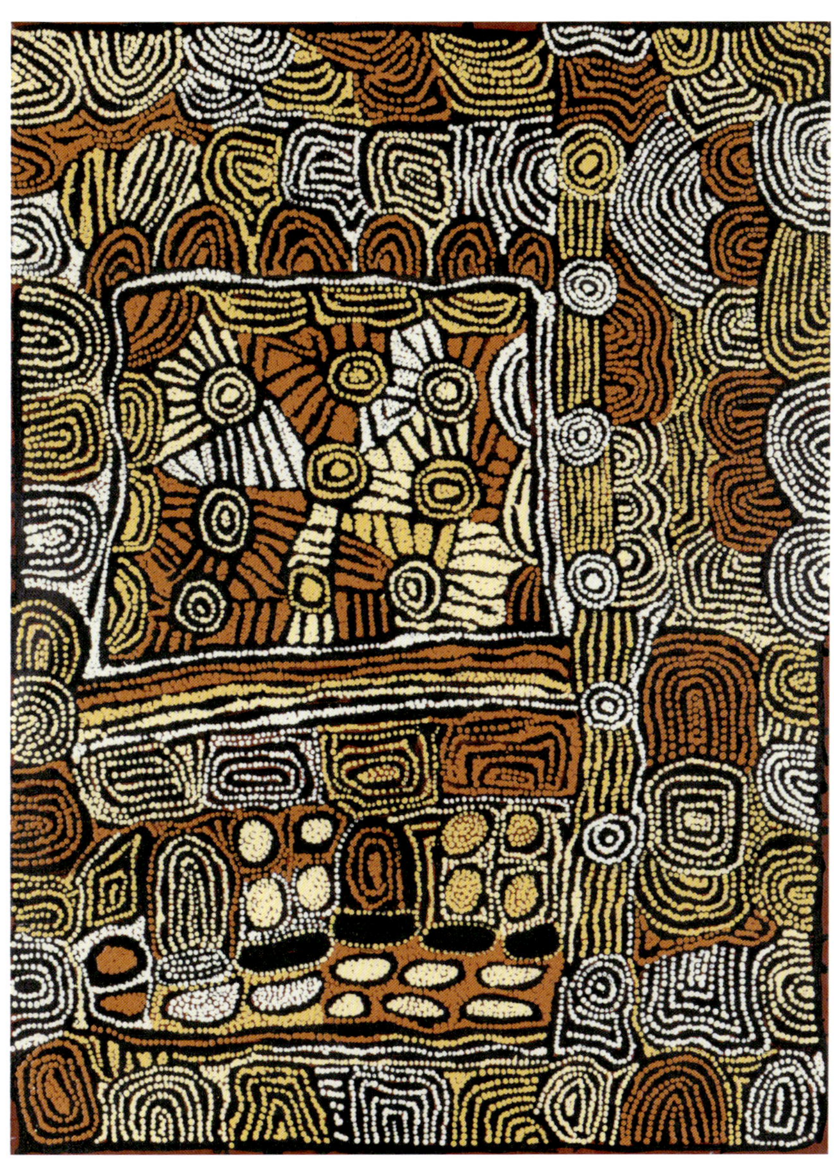

Kapi Tjukurrpa, 2010

Acrylic on Belgian linen, 122 × 91 cm
Philippson Collection

BILL WHISKEY TJAPALTJARRI

Bill Whiskey Tjapaltjarri (ca. 1920–2008) belongs to the Pirupa Akla community around Mount Liebig, west of Uluru. All his life, the artist would call this region "arrogant white country" in reference to the immaculate cliffs that struck his imagination. As a child, his family migrated to Uluru to find food and water, and they came into contact with white culture while pursuing a nomadic lifestyle based on hunting. In his early twenties, Bill Whiskey Tjapaltjarri moved to Haasts Bluff to work as a cook for the Lutheran mission while learning to be a traditional healer (*Ngangkari*). His full black beard and whiskers earned him the nickname "Whiskey".

Having settled with his family in Amanturrungu, near Mount Liebig, he started to paint in 2004, at the age of eighty-four. His favourite themes at that time were the cliffs and caves of Pirupa and Uluru, as well as the stories of his own peregrinations in Areyonga and Haasts Bluff. His painting is marked by a vivid sense of colour that reflects a spirit of boldness and vital energy. The tight weave of his "pointillism" with its white layers gives his Tachisme an immediately recognisable depth of field. Bill Whiskey Tjapaltjarri went on to gain dazzling recognition although his work, spanning less than five years, remains scarce.

His traditionally inspired painting tells the story of the creation of the great sacred sites and often features the story of three mythical birds. *Rockholes and Country near the Olgas* recounts how the Eagle saved the Cockatoo Ancestor from the attacks of the Raven, who was tempted by the large white larvae essential to its survival. With its dazzling white rocks, the site is the birthplace of the Ancestor whose constant presence and attention have allowed the cockatoo to thrive. In the painting, the large white masses reflect the location and the mythical animal at the same time. Mount Connor is depicted by certain lines, while the red and yellow dots represent the flowers that grow on the site and which form the essential food of the cockatoo. The concentric circles represent the birthplace of the bird. As one of the last works of the artist, this piece is no longer bound by the need to portray the tale through its figures. The Eagle, the Cockatoo and the Raven are not shown, but the whole symbolic terrain refers to the mythical story enshrined in the "Dreamtime".

40

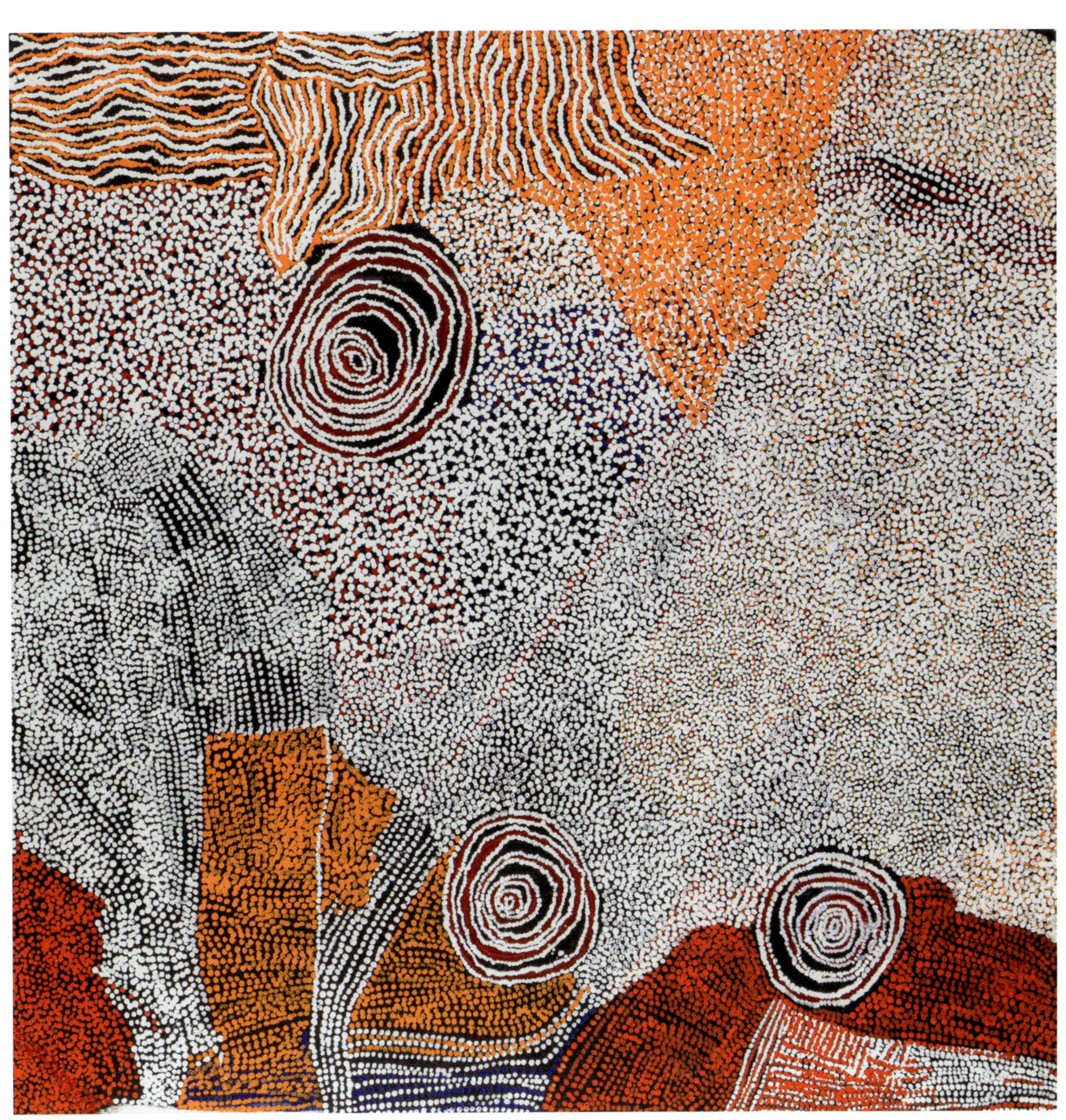

Rockholes and Country near the Olgas, 2008

Acrylic on linen, 153 × 154 cm
Philippson Collection

In this piece, Jonathan Kumintjarra Brown (1960–1997) takes painting back to its ritual origins: a symbolic line drawn on the ground with the end of a stick and destined to be erased after the ceremony is over. It thereby recalls the topographical foundation of the canvas as a place where timeless symbolic knowledge emerges. The black and white concentric circles repeated in the Pitjantjatjara settings, which are connected by lines and linked to each other in large pointillist patches, are here brought back to their primary expression. However, in reference to the state of nuclear devastation associated with the painter's region of origin (the Maralinga landscape was the site of nuclear tests between 1956 and 1967), the representation can be interpreted in the opposite direction when linked to other paintings from the same series: for example, *Old Country – Maralinga Atomic Test* (1995) features the same composition, but the central circle appears atomised, the ground irradiated, its heart devastated. Ritual timelessness responds to nuclear devastation: dry and dead earth has covered the image, veiling its faded colours, obscuring any lines that convey ancestral knowledge, thus shattering any future transmission.

In reality, both readings intersect. The very title, *Broad Shield Design*, is an invitation: the concentric patterns refer to shield decorations. They symbolise protection and the promise of a rebirth that would restore immutability to the "Dreamtime" (*tjukurrpa*). There is life on the other side of death, and for Jonathan Brown Kumintjarra, this life is a promise of beauty. Through this series of works, the artist provides a silent protest that is unique in the Aboriginal painting repertoire. Tragedy is not relegated to a mythical time, which is by definition removed from all real events. Even atomised, the *tjukurrpa* persists, if only in the ochre of the earth that bears all painting.

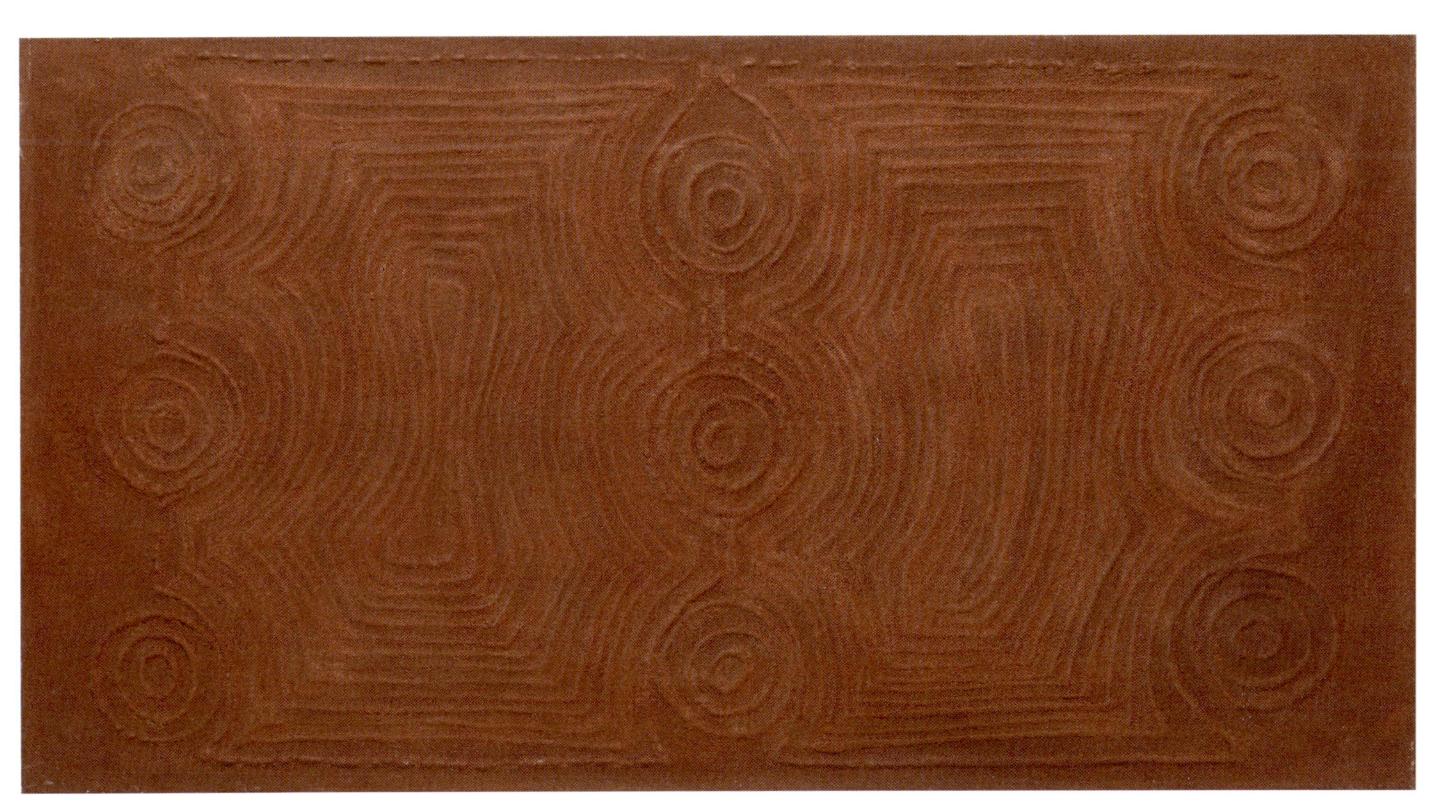

Broad Shield Design, 1996

Ochre on linen, 101 × 193 cm
Philippson Collection

This second piece by Jonathan Kumintjarra Brown characterises the works produced in the wake of Papunya Tula. It reflects the Pitjantjatjara imagination and bears witness to the tragic conditions of Aborigenality after the Second World War. The painter was born in 1960 and was taken away from his mother to be placed in an urban foster home. After much research, he was able to trace his family and community of origin, which he joined in the early 1980s. He then found out that his home area of Maralinga in the South Australian hinterland had been the site of nuclear tests carried out between 1953 and 1967 by the British Army. In a series of seven explosions and more than 600 "spot tests", the southern Great Victoria Desert landscape was reduced to a wasteland. So much so, that for Aborigines the name "Maralinga" — which referred to thunder — is now used to label this chapter of Australian history.

Through the theme of the Emu Ancestor — whose death is represented here by the inclusion of feathers in the charred, irradiated earth — his work reflects the devastation of nature. This explains the contrast between the symbolic zones made up of concentric circles and lines circling the dotted areas of the ancestral ritual with the centre of the painting, which is Matterist in style, glazed by heat a thousand times greater than that of the sun. Although critical in a way that Aboriginal art seldom is, the message is not inherently nihilistic. Despite the desolation, a certain structure reclaims its rights through the layers of superimposed colour, returning the world to its original coherence.

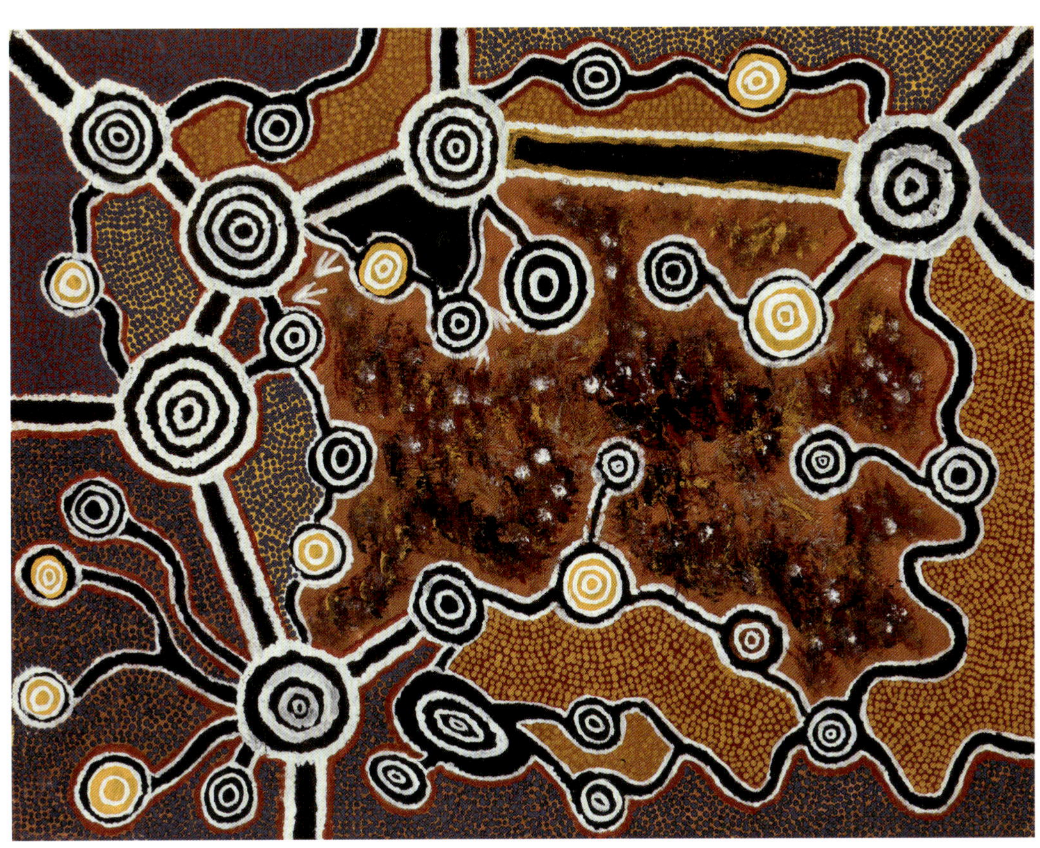

Maralinga – Dead Emus, 1992

Pigment, emu feathers on panel, 71 × 92 cm
Philippson Collection

TIMOTHY WULANJBIRR

Until the artists of Panunya Tula laid the foundations of an increasingly widely recognised "contemporary Aboriginal art", the majority of figurative Aboriginal painting was produced by populations occupying the Northern Territories, which were the last to be colonised. Using natural pigments, they painted on cut and flattened eucalyptus bark or on hollowed-out trunks known as *lorrkkons*. Again, in the context of the missions set up within the communities, the emergence of a local economy based on the production of these paintings gave rise to a craft that has continued to expand, initially targeting rare travellers and tourists before enjoying ever wider recognition. In this respect, the research carried out by ethnologists will help to contextualise these representations which all involve the "Dreamtime".

Born into a family of renowned artists in the Balgo community and the Dangkorlo clan, Timothy Wulanjbirr (ca. 1969) follows this tradition. In the wake of John Mawurndjul, he excels in the practice of *rarrk*: a pattern of polychrome cross-hatching through which the Ancestor's presence comes to life, lending it a certain brightness through which the painter also conveys the tropical climate. The latter is at the heart of the painting, defining the ecosystem to which the Dangkorlo clan belongs. Climate rhymes with landscape, giving context to the ritual action that guides the painting. In Timothy Wulanjbirr's work, figurative representation tends to disintegrate into abstraction through its linear treatment. The *Rainbow Serpent* — an archetypal figure at the heart of the "Dreamtime"— demonstrates the artist's characteristic finesse of execution and precise lines. Conceptual intensity and aesthetic sense merge and, in this way, the artist revives the tradition of the Dangkorlo clan of Arnhem Land.

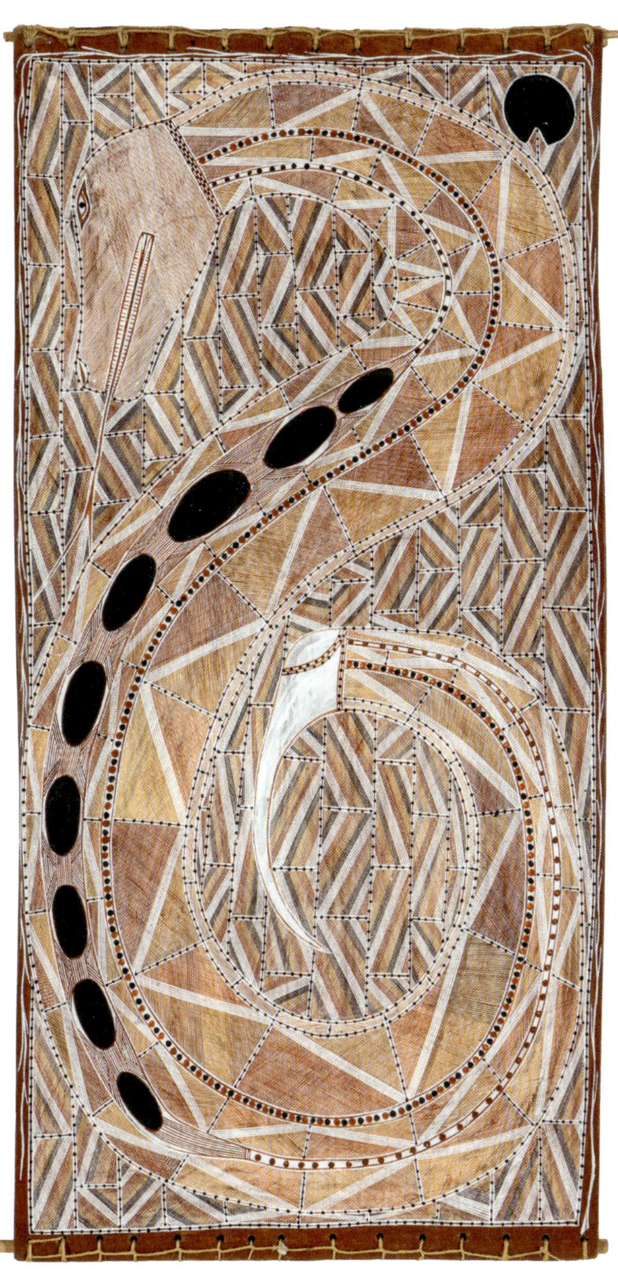

Ngalyod the Rainbow Serpent, 2001

Natural pigment on eucalyptus bark, 108 × 54 cm
Philippson Collection

47

TIMOTHY COOK MARNTUPUNI

Born on Melville Island, Timothy Cook Marntupuni (ca. 1958) is a prominent artist of the North Arnhem Islands. As a member of the Jilamara Arts & Crafts Association, he has gained recognition as a painter and sculptor with his *lorrkkons*. His work is closely affiliated with aspects of Tiwi ceremony and particularly Kulama and Pukumani burial rites. Enjoying a rapidly growing reputation, Timothy Cook has established himself as one of the most radical interpreters of ancient practices as collected by Charles Mountford in 1954 and now displayed at the South Australian Museum in Adelaide. The artist reinterprets forms archived by museums and incorporates them into traditional songs and dances to produce a performative representation in much the same spirit as the artworks still executed in the Tiwi Islands today. The piece on display is based on the Pukumani funeral ritual: several months after the funeral, ornate poles are planted on the burial site following a ceremony involving song and dance. These poles are then left untouched to be destroyed by nature. For the Aboriginalities exhibition, Timothy Cook's *Tutini and Tunga* is presented between two poles carved from acacia trunks by Dhuwarrwarr Marika (*Yalanbara-Larrakitji, Hollow Dog*, 2020, left) and Malaluba Gumana (*Garrimala*, 2007, right), two women artists from Yirrkala.

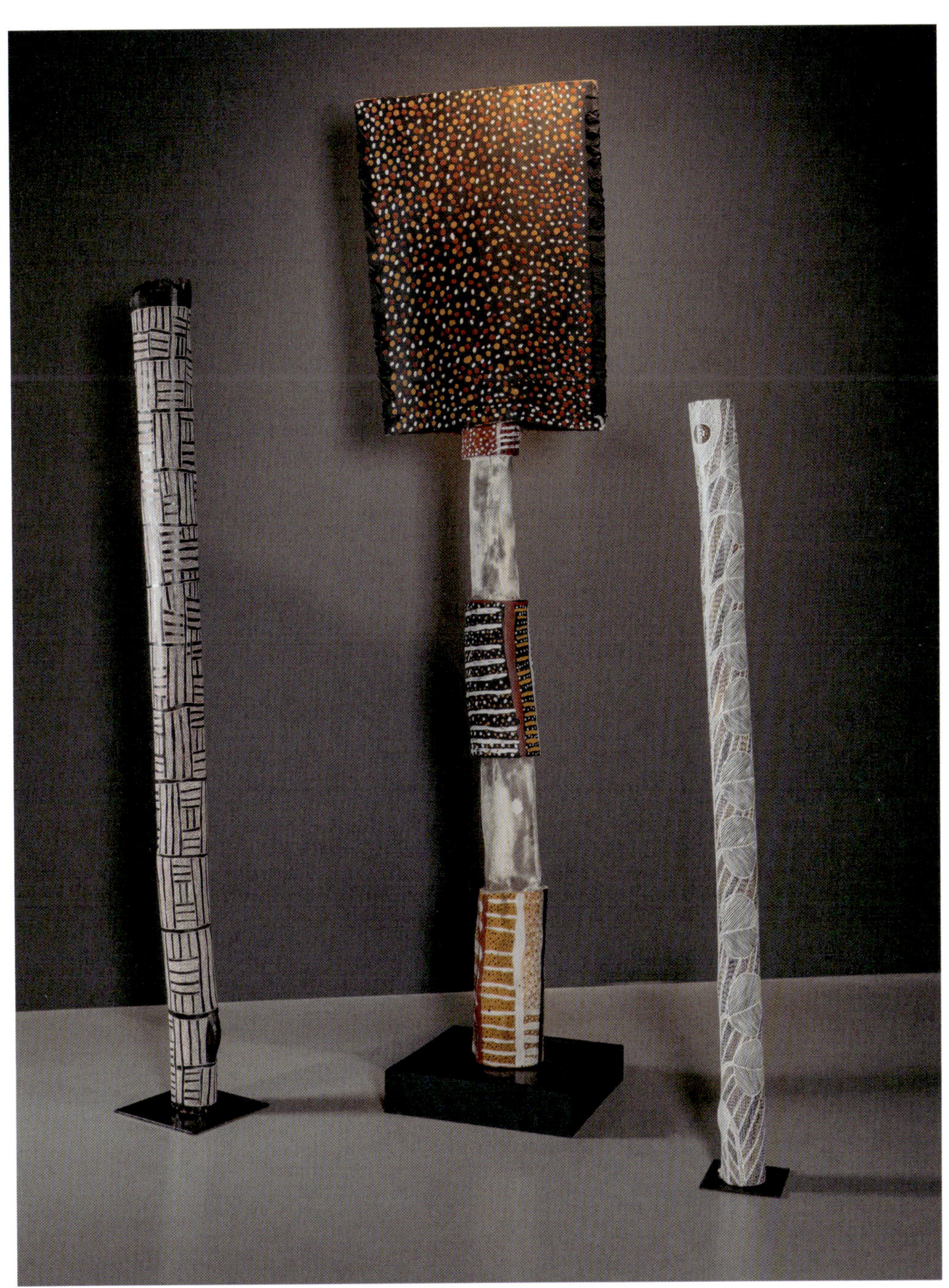

Center: Timothy Cook Marntupuni – *Untitled (Tutini and Tunga)*, 2007

Natural pigment on ironwood, height: 260 cm
Philippson Collection

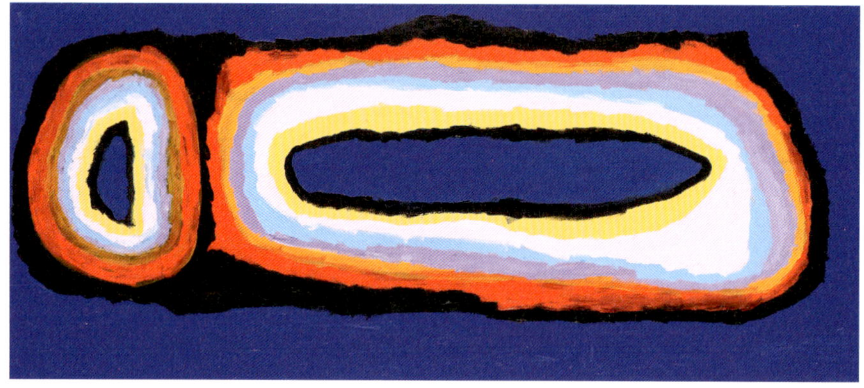

Big Crocodile, 2005
Acrylic on canvas, 91 × 210 cm, Philippson Collection

Sally Gabori, whose tribal name is Mirdidingkingathi Juwarnda (i.e. the dolphin born in Mirdidingkingathi), is from Bentinck Island in the Gulf of Carpentaria, north-east of Darwin. She was a member of the Kaiadilt ethnic group and enjoyed a traditional lifestyle far away from the Western sphere of influence. The traditional community lived from fishing and foraging but was displaced by missionaries to Mornington Island in the 1940s. Sally Gabori was too old to receive an education and never learned to read or write.

In the piece *Big Crocodile*, which she painted at the age of 81, she demonstrates a non-figurative gestural energy. In reality, the gesture takes on essential significance. Through it, the experience acquired is enshrined in traditional representations: traditional landscapes, land or sea, inhabited by figures from the "Dreamtime", such as this marine Crocodile Ancestor. This ancestral subject matter is echoed by a sense of colour and execution reflecting a feminine sensibility that links her to the creations of Minnie Pwerle or Emily Kame. The internationally acclaimed work of Sally Gabori is proof of change in Aboriginal art, which, without severing its ancestral roots, finds new forms of expression.

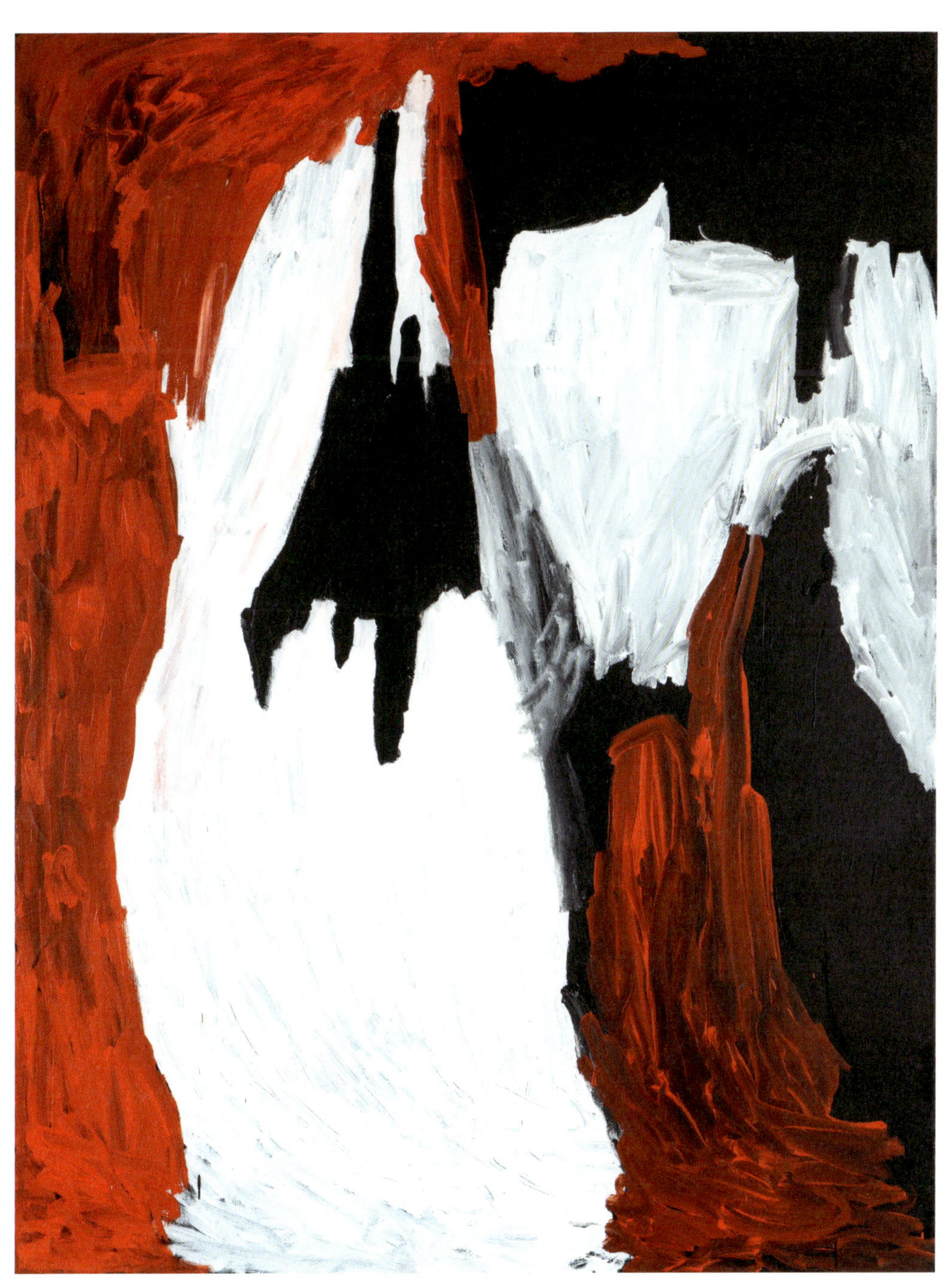

Dibirdibi Country, 2012

Acrylic on canvas, 197 × 150 cm
Philippson Collection

Regina Pilawuk Wilson (ca. 1945) grew up in the Daly Catholic Mission, established south of Darwin in the late 19th century. The ban on speaking one's own language and the pressure exerted by the Jesuits to honour one's ancestors and make baskets as all of them had done, made life extremely painful. Regina fled the mission in 1969 with her husband and a group of people, to her native land. They founded a community at Peppimenarti (meaning "big rock"), 300 kilometres south-west of Darwin. Here, they went back to their roots, restoring ritual ceremonies and, for Regina Pilawuk Wilson, practising basketry.

During the Pacific Arts Festival organised in Noumea in 2000, she was introduced to painting. For the artist, this medium allowed her to record the distinctive patterns of basketry in a less random manner than the fabrication of objects destined to disappear over time. In converting this practice, she also asserted the dignity of a skill usually associated with women. In 2003, this process earned her the Telstra National Indigenous and Torres-Strait Islander Art Award.

Recognised as a major figure in Aboriginal art, Regina Pilawuk Wilson promotes a craft-inspired practice and reaffirms a feminine aesthetic that is under-represented and under-appreciated in the art world. Thus, her paintings evoke circular "sun carpets" that can unfold into cones to become garments or baskets, or nets with a weave that mixes delicate tones with the solidity of a fundamental structure. Her patterns are based on the mesh and weave of fishing nets (*syaw* in Ngangikurrungurr). Here we find reference to the techniques used by women to weave bags and baskets from the vine fibres of the bush that thrive on riverbanks. Moreover, the weaving pattern also invokes some of the body decorations used for certain ceremonies practised by women, as can be seen in the work *Woman's Body Painting* by Abie Loy Kemarre (see p. 64).

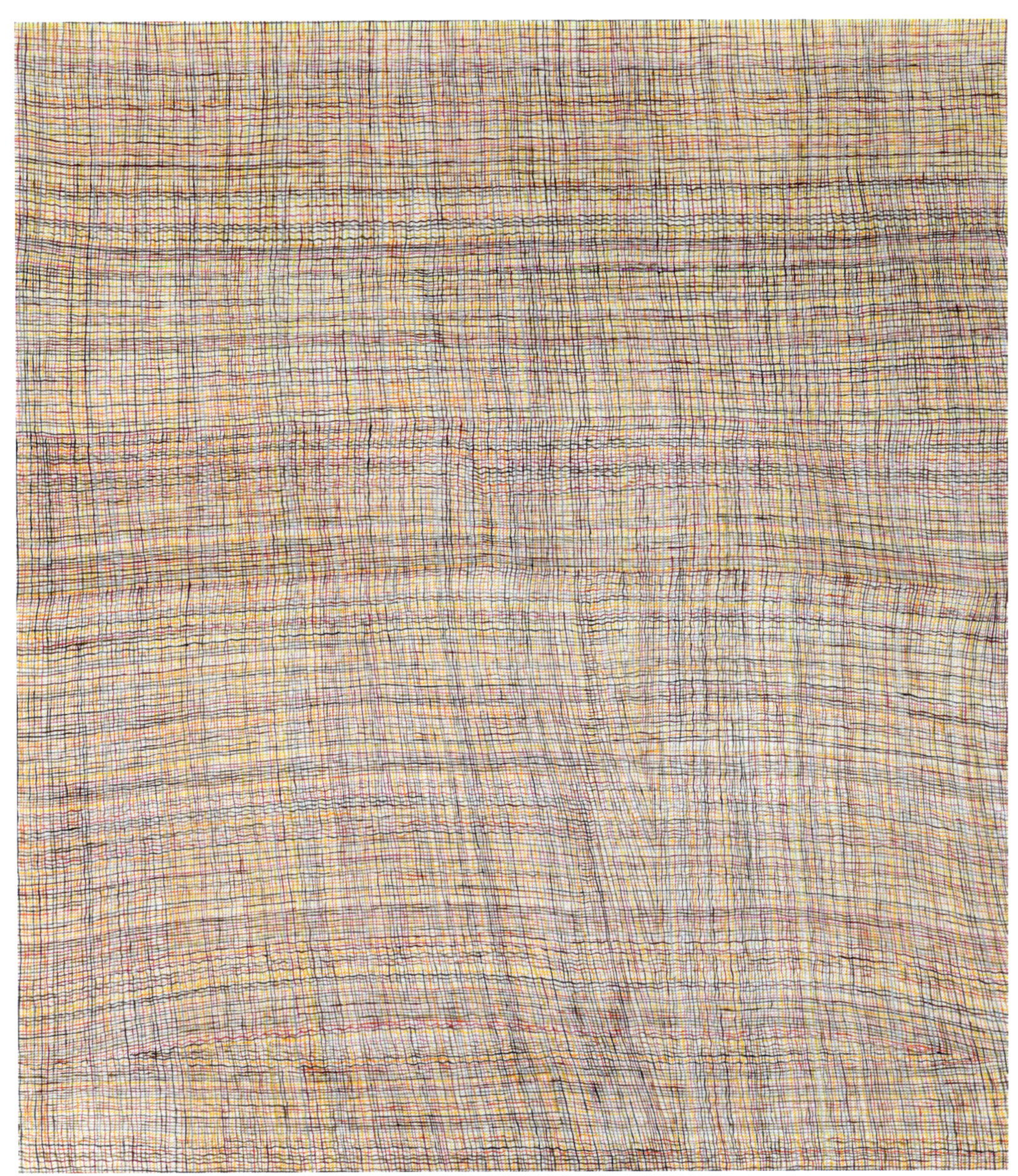

Syaw (Fish net), 2002

Acrylic on canvas, 138 × 124 cm
Philippson Collection

EMILY KAME KNGWARREYE

Emily Kame Kngwarreye (1910–1996) is a major figure in Aboriginal art. Born in Utopia, she first began working with batik. This demanding fabric printing technique had a profound effect on her visual imagination. In the early 1980s, she turned to painting and developed a personal style that emerged from the rigorous pointillism of Papunya Tula. Emily Kane gives Aboriginal cosmogony a sensuousness that serves as a declaration of independence for a feminine interpretation of the tradition. By using the effects of braiding or the patterns of body decorations worn by women during rituals, she opens new perspectives.

In a piece entitled *Anooralya Yam Awelye*, she depicts the life cycle of a food plant. This tuber is essential to the survival of the community and is grown in the Alalgura region, near the Utopia station. Her painting gives an aerial view of the growth of this plant, which sprouts in clusters after the summer rains, when the flow of water restores the Alalgura basin and the river gains increasing speed as it gushes forth. The seed-bearing flowers of the *anooralya yam* are called Kame — which is the tribal name adopted by the artist who identifies with the flower. In the cracks that run through the ground, the plant reveals a presence that will become reality as long as the ceremonies continue to be held and the ritual performed. Emily Kame's brother, Kudditji Kngwarreye, is also a painter.

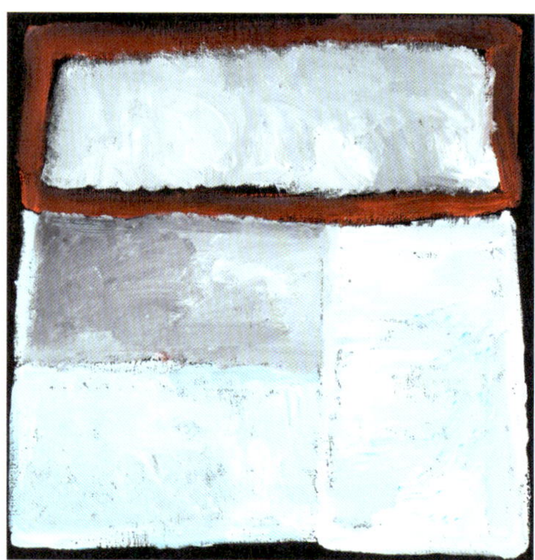

Kudditji Kngwarreye
My Country, 2013

Acrylic on canvas, 60 × 60 cm
Philippson Collection

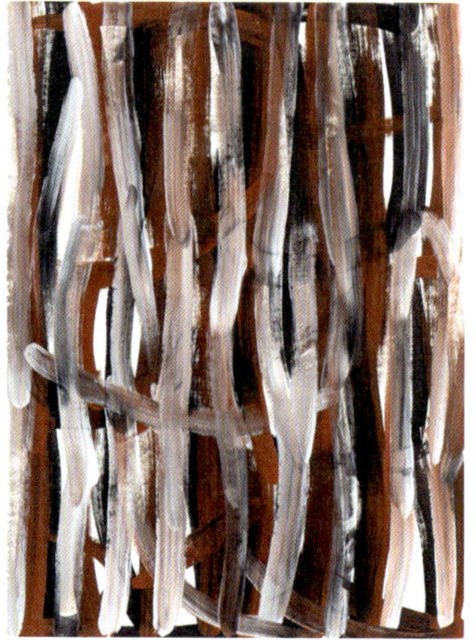

Emily Kame Kngwarreye
Body Paint, 1995

Acrylic on paper, 76 × 51 cm
Philippson Collection

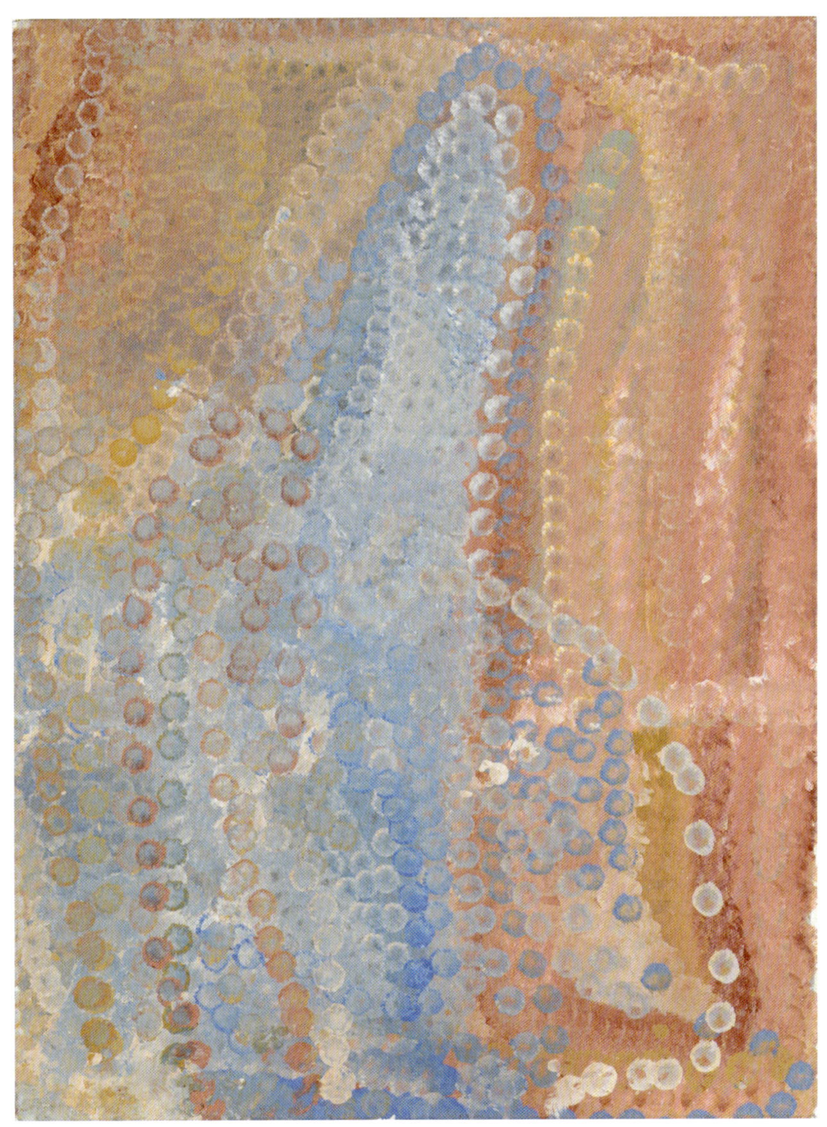

Anooralya Yam Awelye, 1994

Acrylic on linen, 90 × 70 cm
Philippson Collection

Minnie Pwerle (ca. 1915–2006) was born in Utopia, an Aboriginal community some 350 kilometres north-east of Alice Springs. Two closely related language communities are clustered around the Sandover River: the Anmatyerre and the Alyawarre. In the 1970s, in the wake of the Right to Land policy, the Aborigines regained ownership of this area, where settlers had built an intensive livestock farm. Minnie Pwerle grew up in this context. Responsible for the territory of Atwengerrp, she organised the Awelye ceremonies to ensure the fertility of the land. Right up until her death, the artist drew inspiration from the symbolic designs used during these rites, particularly the motifs used by women to adorn their bodies during the rituals associated with the "Dreams" of Atwengerrp: "Dream of Melon Seed" and "Dream of Watermelon". Thus, these paintings are intended to represent the sensations, impressions, visions, and experiences of these ancestral rituals.

The transition to painting and public revelation of this initiatory imagination was not straightforward. It was not until 1999 that Minnie Pwerle took the plunge, even though the painters of Utopia had been working on the subject from 1977. Her paintings instantly express vitality and energy, conveyed through colour. Through her confident lines, Minnie Pwerle reveals a spontaneous vision, marked by a subjectivity that is uncommon in traditional Aboriginal art. In the tangled web of large iridescent arabesques, the woman relives her "Melon Dream" more than she narrates it.

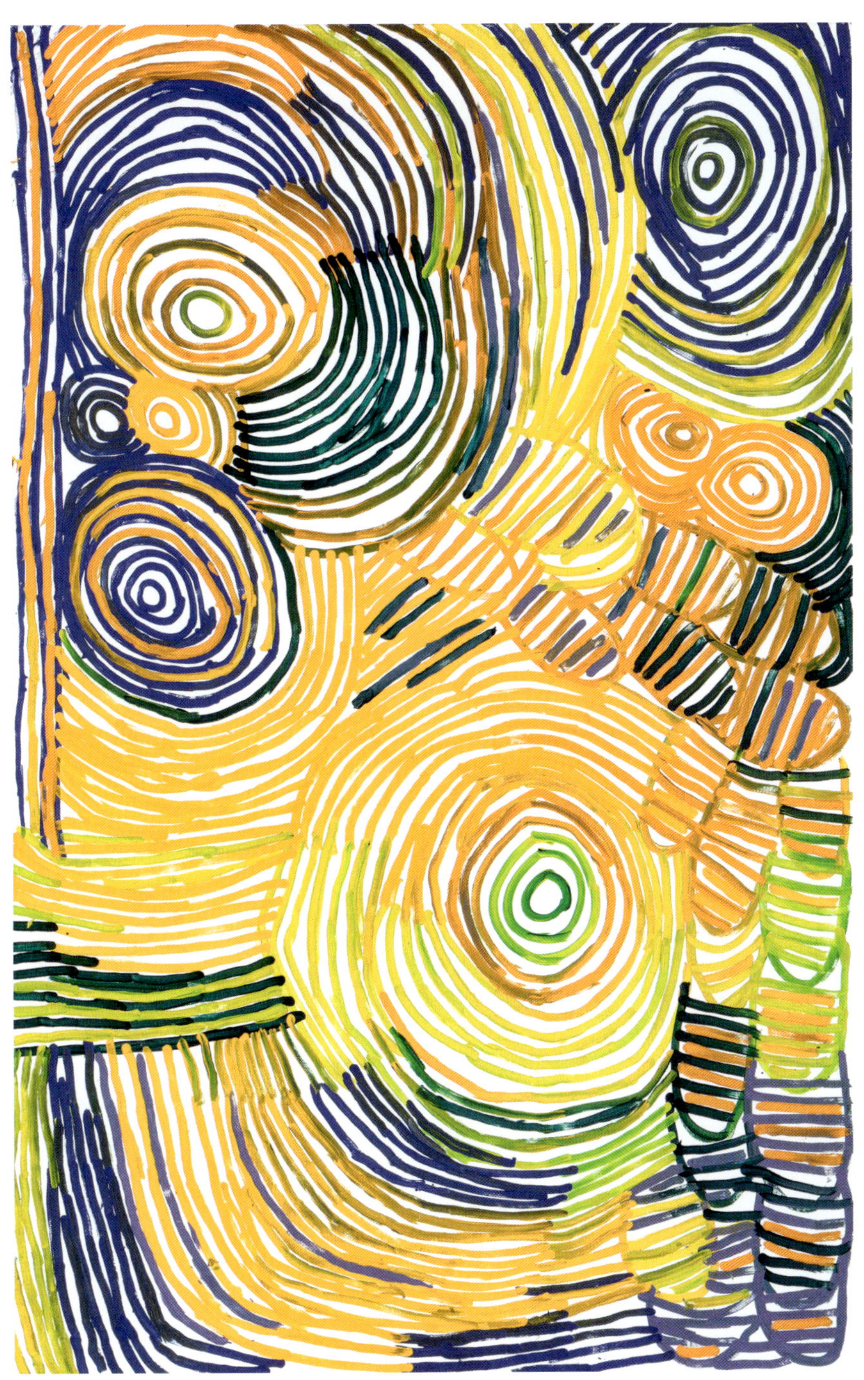

Bush Melon

Acrylic on canvas, 180 × 120 cm
Philippson Collection

KATHLEEN PETYARRE

Born less than 300 kilometres north of Alice Springs, Kathleen Petyarre (ca. 1940–2018; her Aboriginal name is Kweyetwemp) grew up in the Atnangker region, renowned for the grasses that permeate the landscape. As a native Anmatyer-speaker, she lived a nomadic existence with her large family, moving from waterhole to waterhole in a constant quest for food. These continual migrations were her schooling; she learned to find her way in the desert, to move around, and to find the means to survive in a way that was always frugal and respectful of nature. It was also during these journeys that she was initiated into the traditions linked to the "Dreamtime".

After settling with her family in Utopia, she played a pivotal role in the Aboriginal Land Rights movement. Active to the point of militancy, her action would prove decisive and, in 1979, would enable the Anmatyerre people to recover their ancestral lands, thus becoming the sole legitimate owners of Utopia. In 1988, she presented her first paintings on the occasion of an exhibition dedicated to Utopia, presented by the Holmes à Court Gallery in Perth.

In this context, her clan is vested with the mission of preserving the heritage of the "Dream of the Lizard" (*Arnkerrth*), through the tales and songs linked to it. Totemically linked to this small desert lizard, Kathleen Petyarre dedicated her pictorial work to its presentation. The asexual *Arnkerrth* (or *Moloch horridus*) lives on the ridges of the desert dunes in the Atnangker region. Just like the chameleon, it blends seamlessly into its environment. Beyond its singular physiognomy that has earned it a demonic epithet, its story refers to its endless wandering in the desert with which it becomes merged. The artist represents it in this context. Without attempting to multiply the symbolic codifications that would be associated with the initiation practices and ceremonies attached to the lizard, she magnifies the monumental magnificence of this landscape "of nothingness" through the lizard, which is more suggested than shown. Belonging to a family with many prominent contributors to the rise of the Utopia school of painting, Kathleen Petyarre lends a minimalist density to these mythical maps where the lizard portrays a symbolic experience of the desert. Here, the "Dreamtime" is not a medium for complex narratives, but the epitome of a site that bears the heritage of the Aboriginal societies that have lived there since the dawn of time.

In fact, *Mountain Devil Lizard Dreaming* is a fragment of a series that, when recomposed, reveals the landscape of Kathleen Petyarre's ancestral land. Alongside the Lizard Dreaming, the artist will also create two other "Dreams" from which her spiritual identity emerges: the Bush Seeds Dreaming and the Green Bean Dreaming. In both cases, she uses the same meticulous technique of an almost minimalist "pointillist" method.

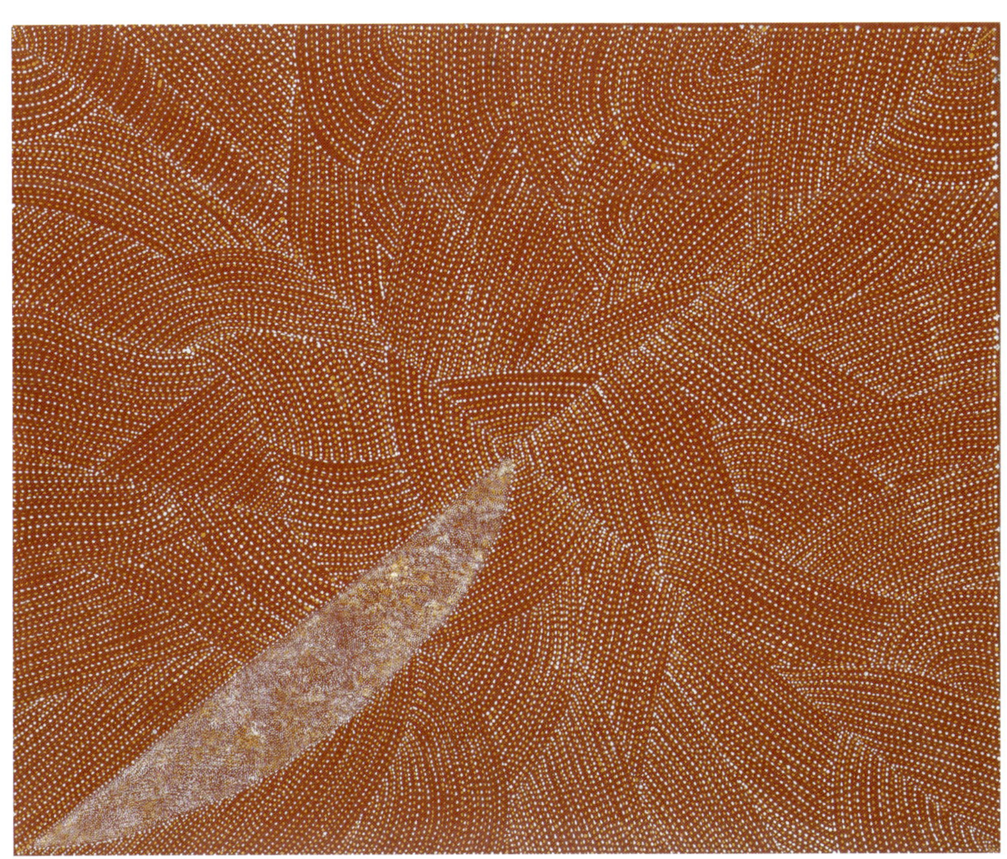

Mountain Devil Lizard, 2012

Acrylic on linen, 95 × 130 cm
Philippson Collection

JOSIE KUNOTH PETYARRE

Josie Kunoth Petyarre (ca. 1959) was born in Alhakere, a community in Central Australia in the Utopia region. An Anmatyerre-speaker, she comes from a family of renowned artists from Utopia: Polly Ngale, Alex Ngwarai as well as her aunts Kathleen and Angelina Ngale. Her siblings — Maisie, Audrey, David and Samy — and her husband Dinni Kemarre have also achieved artistic success.

Like many Aboriginal women, Josie Kunoth Petyarre started painting after many years' practice in batik on silk. In 1989 she turned to painting on canvas for the "Utopia: A Picture Story" project. She produced eighty-eight pieces that were purchased by the Holmes à Court Gallery in Perth. Since 2005, she has also been experimenting with woodcarving in collaboration with her husband. The couple depicts animals and figures as they appear in rituals. The polychromy is vivid, the craftsmanship dynamic. Gradually, both artists have moved away from traditional representations to depict everyday life images — such as the players of the national football team in 2006.

The Sugar Bag series refers to the production of honey by bush bees. The honey is gathered from the trees or from the crevices of rock shelters with baskets made by the community's women. The artist uses the design of these baskets as a pattern to play with formal traditions, without restricting herself to the legendary cycles of the "Dreamtime". In so doing, Josie Kunoth Petyarre introduces a new creative dimension, freeing herself from the exclusive initiation without abandoning her symbolic and formal heritage. Her research is not without a decorative spirit expressed both in her harmony of structure and in the balance of her palette. In this way, she lends a feminine sensibility to an extremely codified art as it emerged after the Papunya Tula adventure.

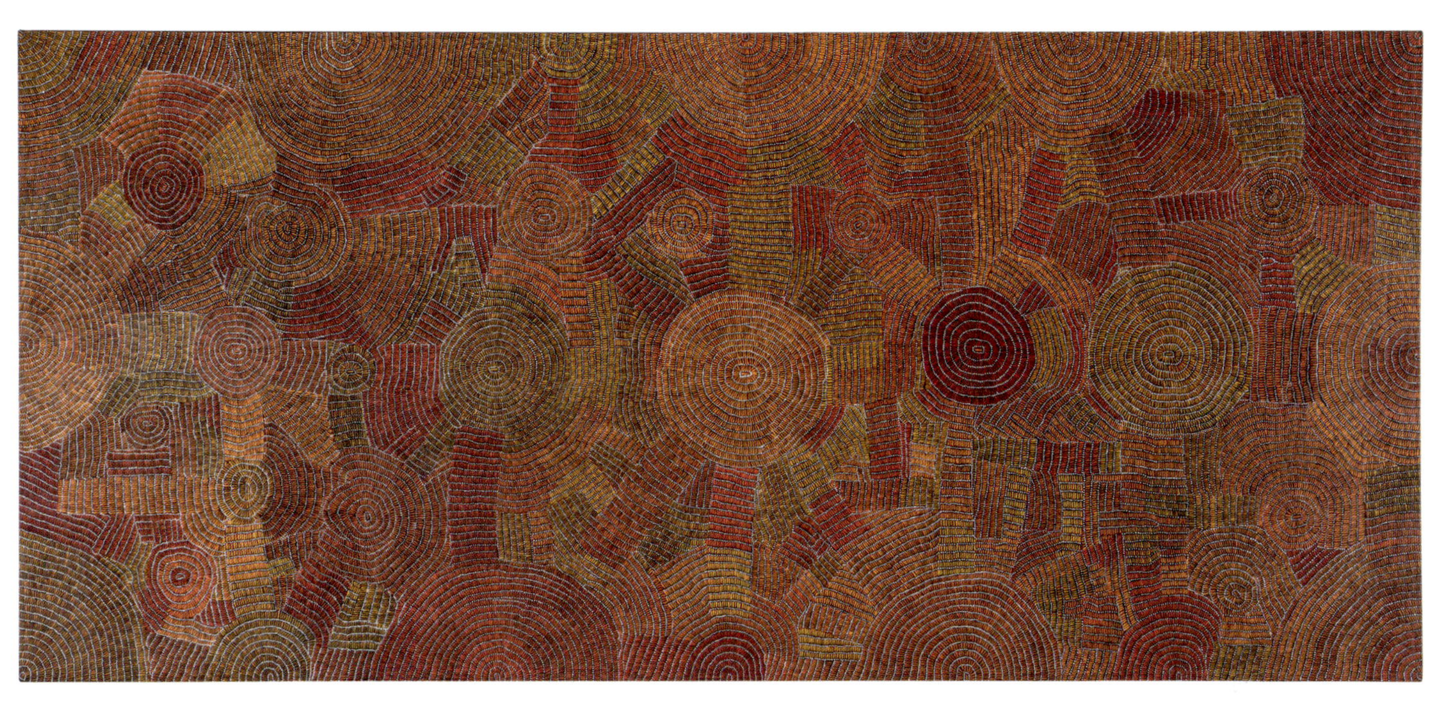

Sugar Bag, 2018

Acrylic on linen, 150 × 350 cm
Philippson Collection

Gloria Tamerre Petyarre (ca. 1940) is one of seven Petyarre sisters who share the same "Dream". She started painting in 1988, first with batik and later with acrylic. *Wild Flowers and Medicinal Leaves* is one of the generic paintings of her *Bush Medicine* series based on the depiction of the medicinal plants flowering in the Central Desert. With the October rains, the usually barren and arid space is covered with vegetation in subtle and fragile hues. Gloria Petyarre's art is primarily devoted to this celebration of the earth, which she expresses through her use of colour, including black and white. The artist never concedes to a multi-coloured impulse based on abundance. There is no symphony of colours, but a monochrome movement traversed from within by hypnotic waves that create the effect of the delicate movement of the wind in the budding new foliage. Sometimes, Gloria Petyarre links this sensation to a few loose leaves in a single supple gesture. Here, her brushwork has tightened to render the presence of each leaf, thereby creating the figurative equivalent of the dot in the classical productions. The leaves form organic entities imbued with a sensual flow that is also the path of the shamanic spirit in the smallest gifts of nature. Combined with rain, this oceanic movement transforms the desert into a source of life.

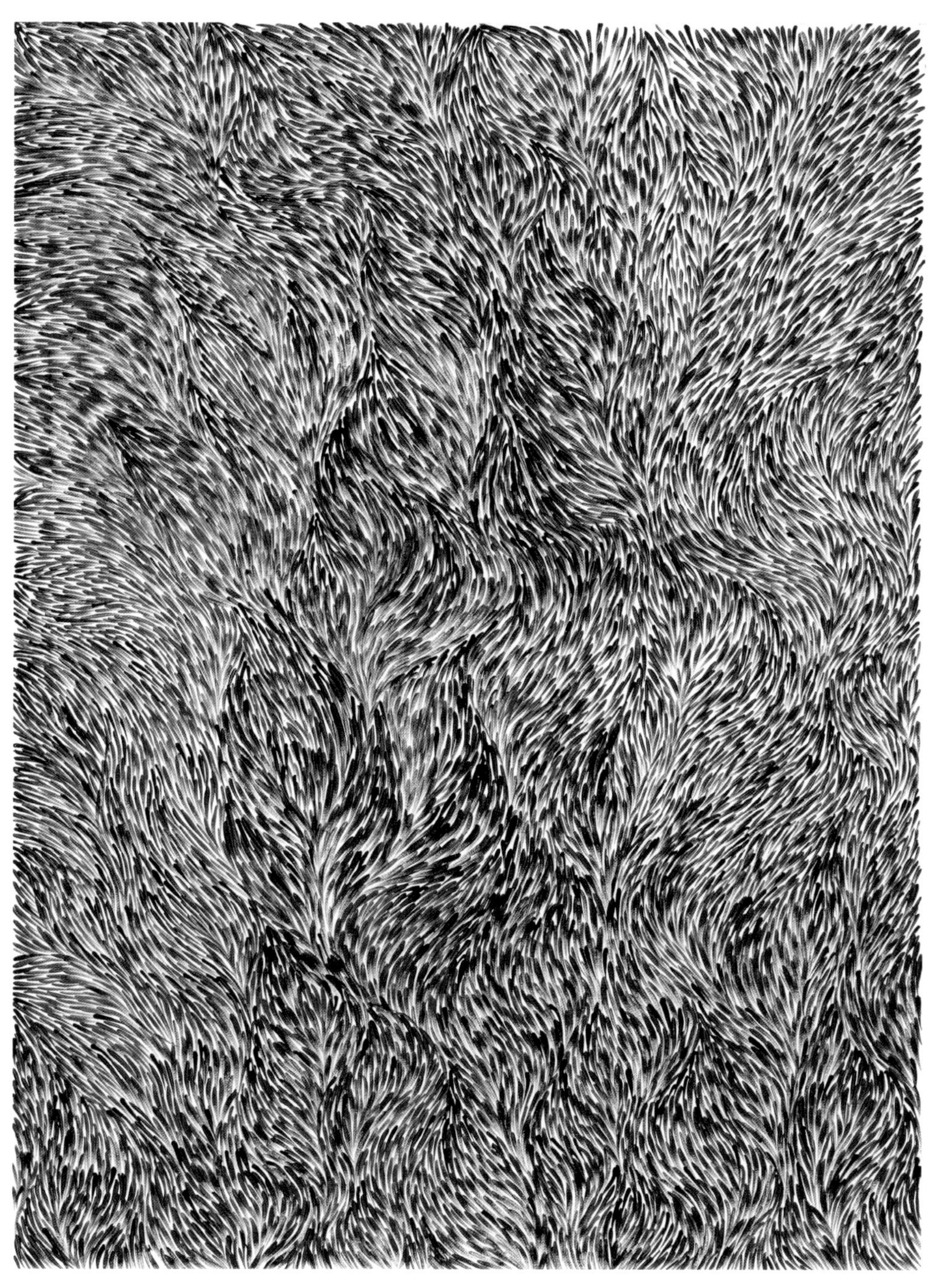

Wild Flowers and Medicine Leaves, 2005

Acrylic on canvas, 182 × 138 cm
Philippson Collection

ABIE LOY KEMARRE

Born in Utopia, Abie Loy Kemarre (ca. 1972) is a member of the Anmatyerre language group. Her grandmother Kathleen Petyarre taught her to paint. The notoriety of her grandmother considerably contributed her own recognition as she regularly accompanies her grandmother on her travels and works at her side as her assistant. However, this has not prevented Abie Loy Kemarre from developing her own style. Three main themes permeate her work: the "Dream of the Bush Leaf", the "Dream of the Bush Hen" and the "Awelye". This piece falls into this category and, (along with Judy Watson Napangardi [see pp. 72–73] and Minnie Pwerle [see pp. 56–57]) demonstrates masterful use of black and white, echoing the edge-to-edge patterns drawn on the body during women's ceremonies held in Utopia. Through consistent but uneven lines and shapes, Abie Loy combines weaving and meshing, revealing a feminine fibre nurtured by minimalism.

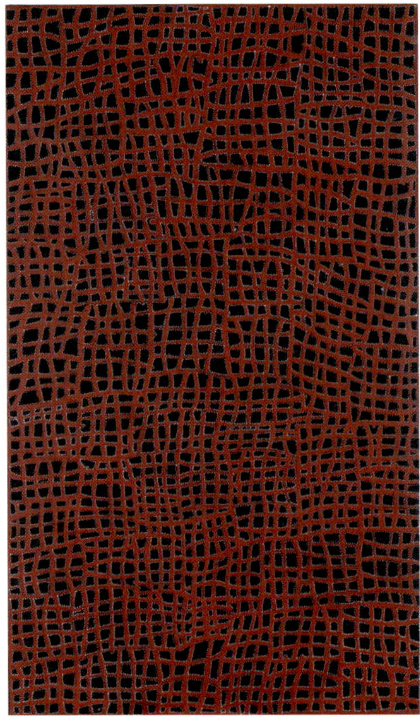

Woman's Body Painting, 2010

Acrylic on canvas, 152 × 90 cm
Philippson Collection

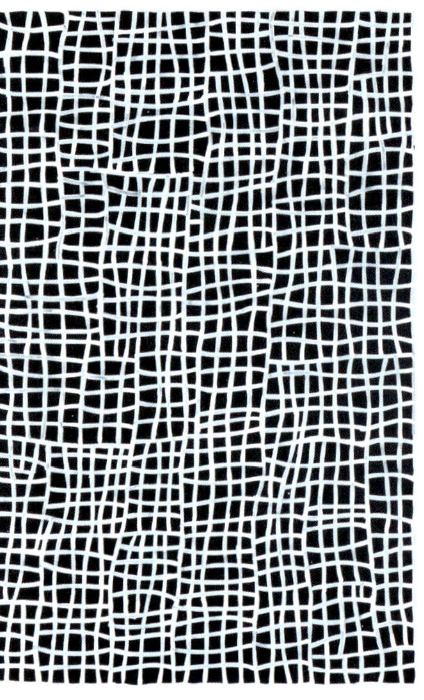

Woman's Body Painting, 2010

Acrylic on canvas, 152 × 90 cm
Philippson Collection

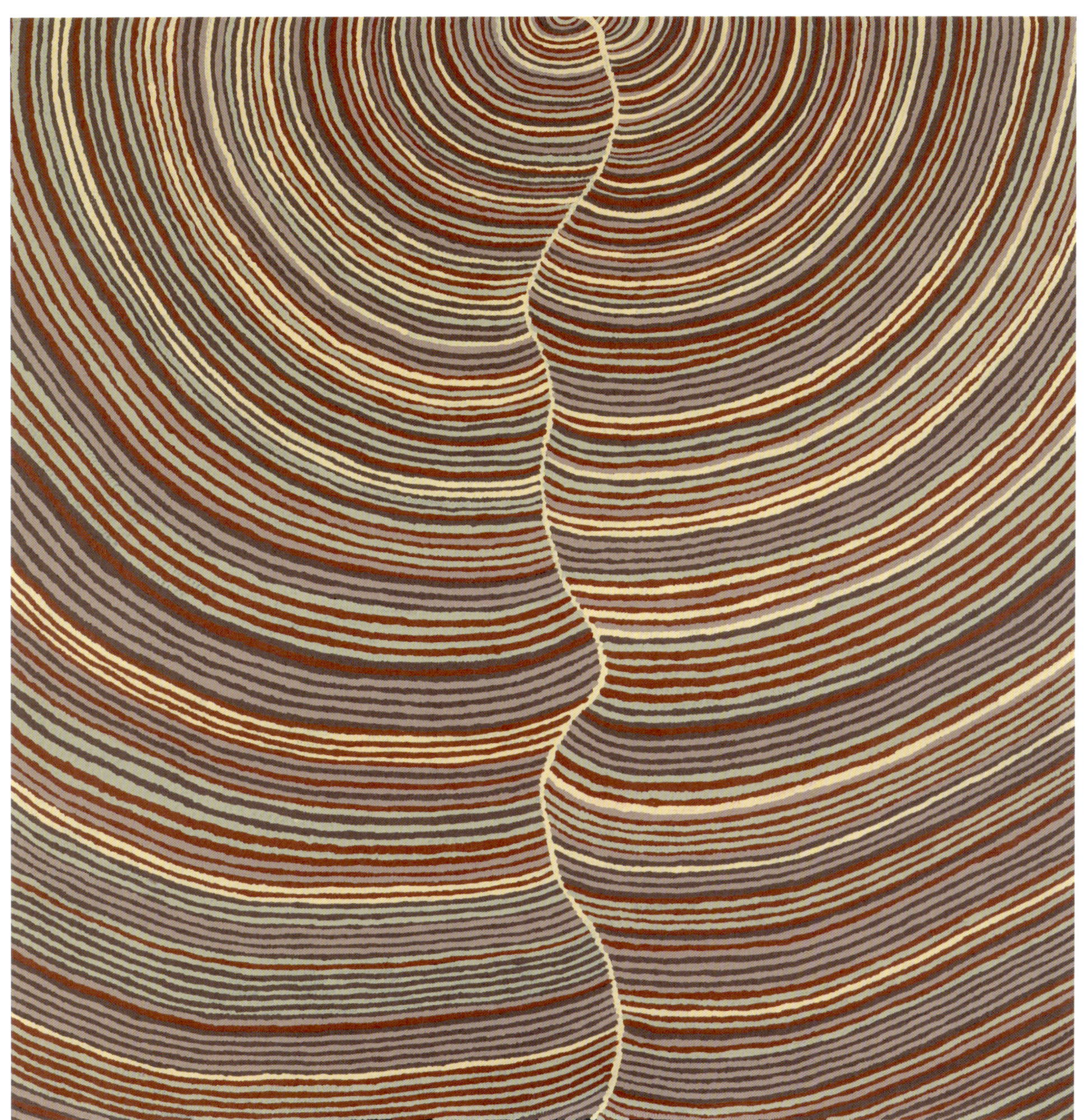

Untitled, 2004

Acrylic on canvas, 151 × 153 cm
Philippson Collection

DEBBIE BROWN NAPALTJARRI

Debbie Napaljarri Brown (ca. 1985) was born in Nyirripi, a remote Aboriginal community 400 kilometres northwest of Alice Springs in the Northern Territory. She was raised and educated there for most of her life, before spending several years at the Yirrara College boarding school in Alice Springs. When she returned to Nyirripi, she worked in a shop, and as a caregiver to the elderly. In 2010, Debbie moved with her husband and son Jarvis to Yuendumu, 160 kilometres further east, to be closer to her husband's family. There she worked for the Women's Centre, preparing lunches for schoolchildren. Introduced to painting by her grandparents, since 2006 she has been involved with the Warlukurlangu Artists Aboriginal Corporation, an indigenous art centre in Yuendumu. Her grandmother, Margaret Napangardi Brown, is also an artist at the same centre. Her grandfather, Pegleg Tjampitjinpa (born ca. 1920), is another renowned Pintupi artist who lived a traditional life in the Wilkinkarra area. In the past, Debbie watched her grandparents paint and listened to her grandmother talk about the *tjukurrpa*. In her paintings, she represents her father's "Dreamtime", which directly refers to her land, its features, plants, and animals. *Tali Tjuta* evokes many of the sand hills walked by the painter's Ancestors.

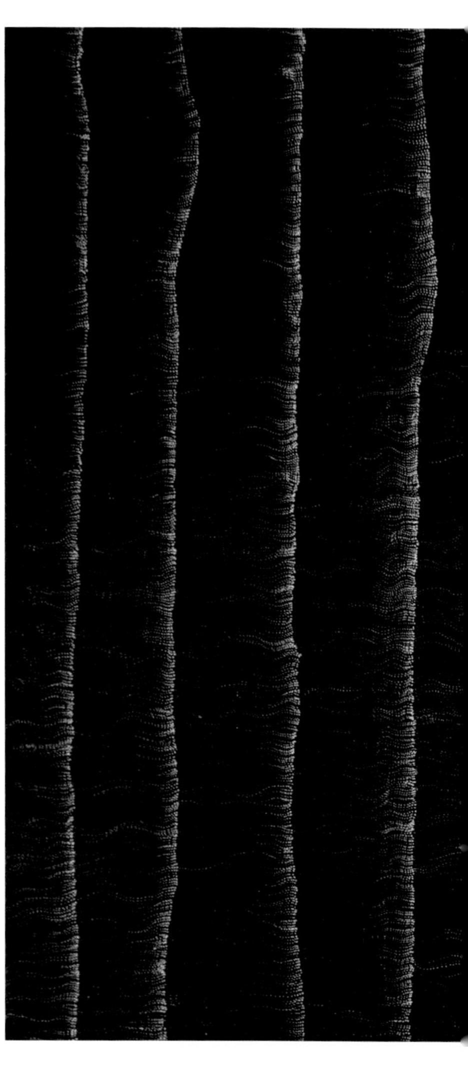

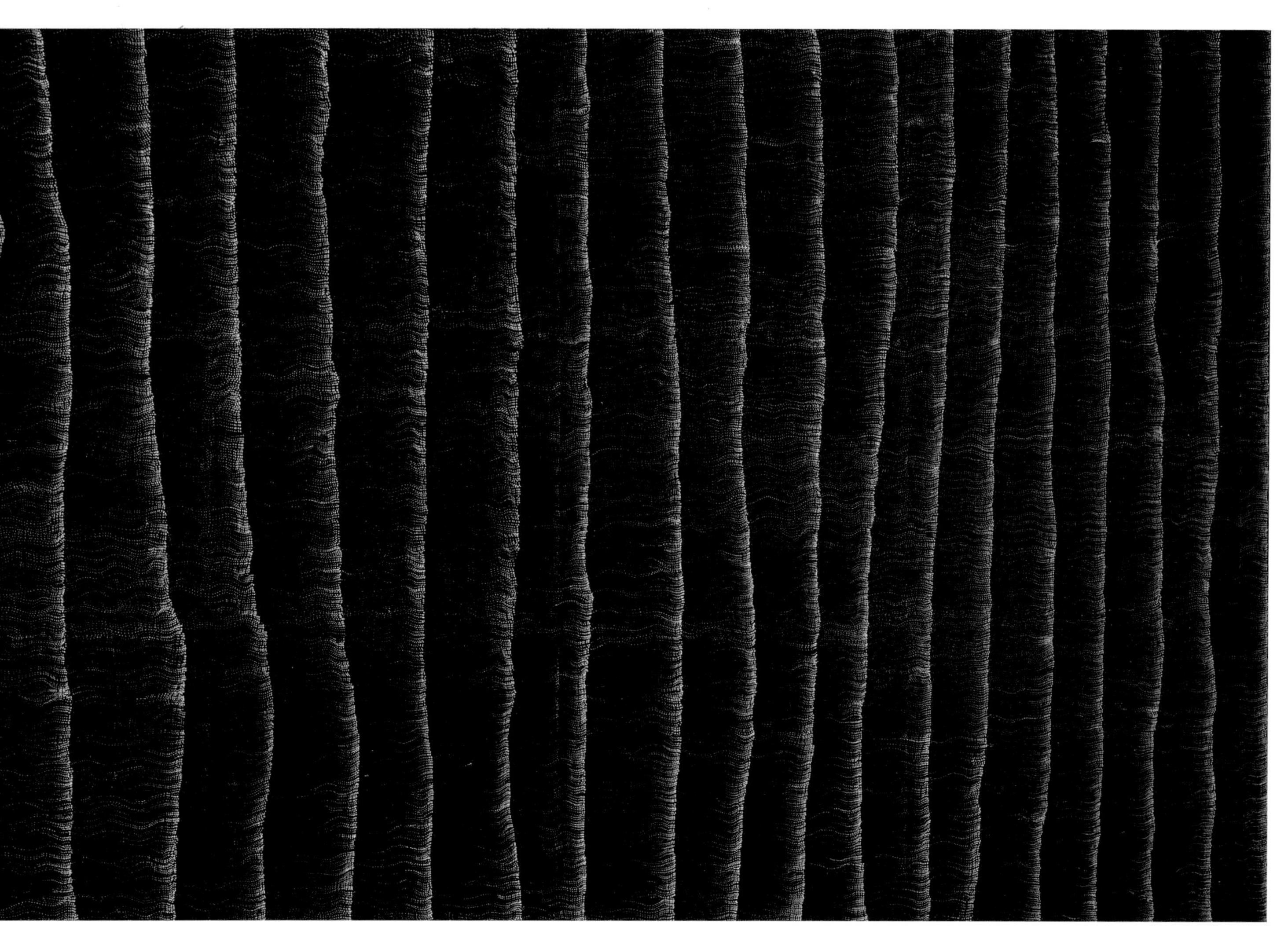

Tali Tjuta (Many Sand Hills), 2019

Acrylic on linen, 244 × 485 cm
RMFAB, donated by Yanda Aboriginal Art, Alice Springs (Australia), 2020, inv. 12597

MARY BROWN NAPANGARDI

Mary Brown Napangardi was born in the Lapi Lapi community, bordering Western Australia and the Northern Territory, 870 kilometres from Alice Springs, in around 1953. Mary's parents led a traditional life in the Mina Mina area between Nyirripi and Lapi Lapi. Both genealogy and geography are prominent in the artist's story: Mina Mina is also the traditional homeland of her extended family, which includes Paddy Lewis Tjapanangka, the father of one of her cousins, Dorothy Napangardi (see p. 70), and Pegleg Tjampitjinpa, Mary's brother-in-law, whose sister he married. In 1957, Mary and her extended family were taken by anthropologist Donald F. Thomson to Mount Doreen, a settlement of 8000 square kilometres.

After the creation of the Nyirripi community (160 kilometres west of Yuendumu, and on the south-western edge of Mount Doreen resort), the family moved once again. Today Mary divides her time between Kintore and Nyirripi with her husband Ronnie Tjampitjinpa (see p. 71).

Mary started painting in the early 1990s, sporadically at first, as there was no art centre where she lived. In 2005, she started working with the Warlukurlangu Artists Aboriginal Corporation in Yuendumu and produced a more consistent body of work. Her compositions incorporate themes and scenes associated with women's ceremonies and the "Dreamtime", pertaining to the land, its motifs, its flora, and fauna. These sacred legends have been passed down from her father's side for generations. Mary uses traditional iconography and an unlimited palette to create a modern interpretation of her dreams.

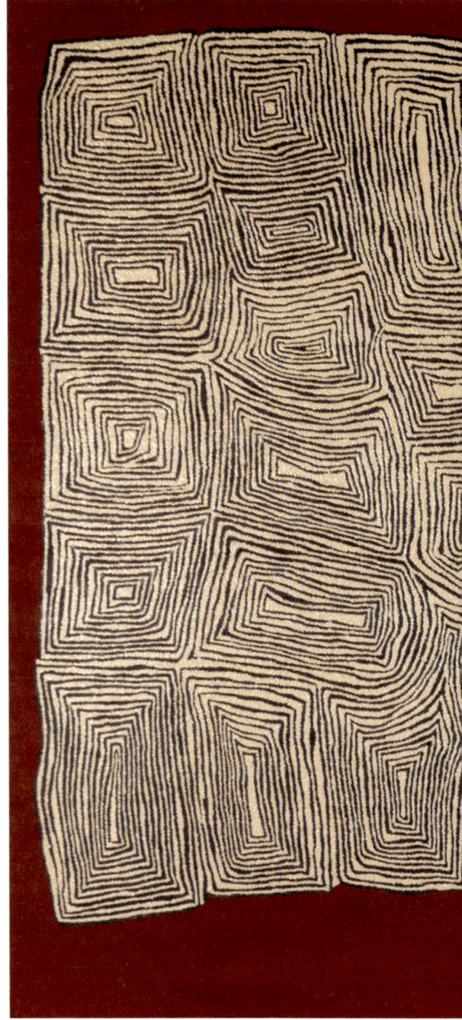

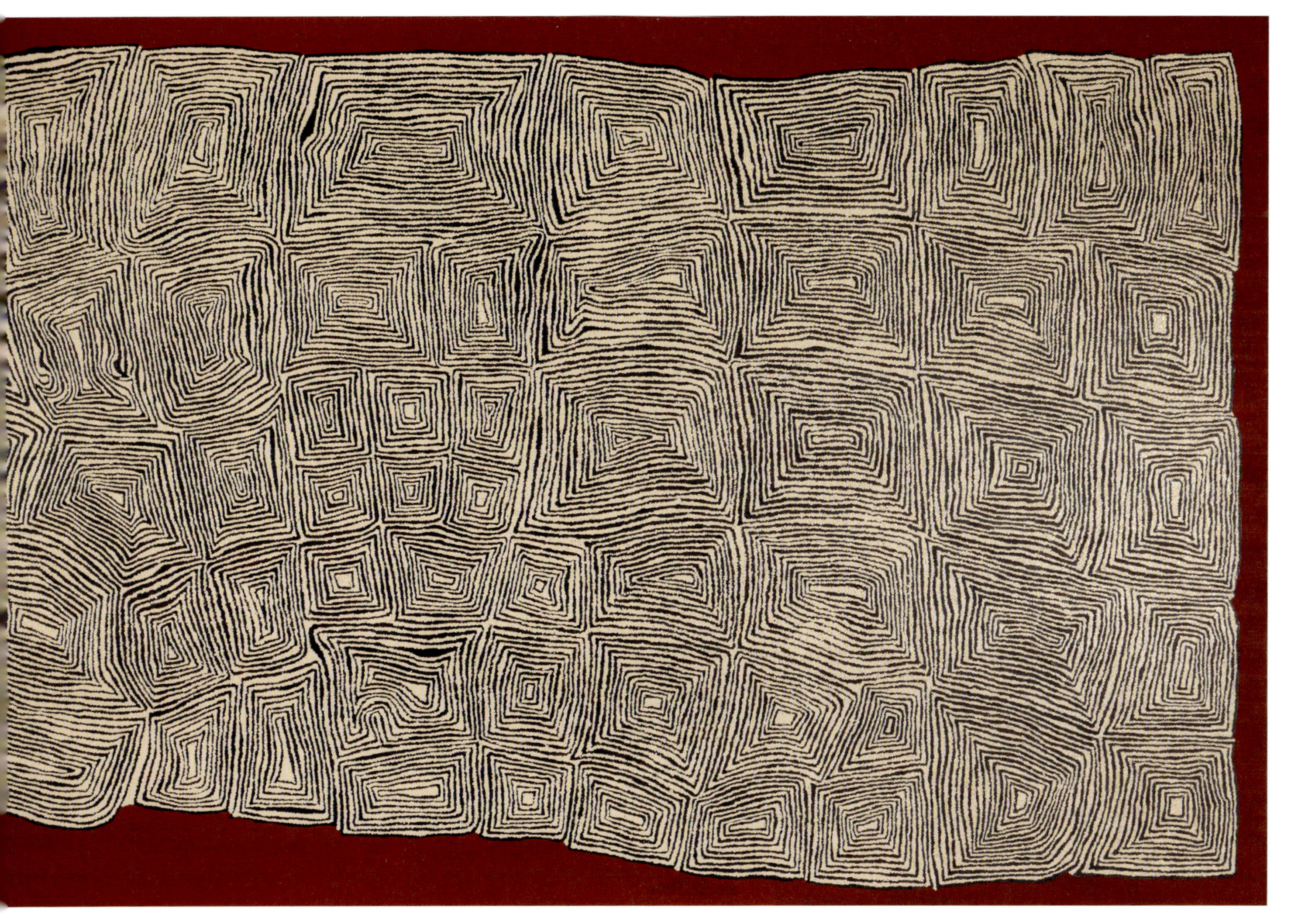

Women's Ceremony, 2019

Acrylic on linen, 244 × 485 cm
RMFAB, donated by Yanda Aboriginal Art, Alice Springs (Australia), 2020, inv. 12598

DOROTHY NAPANGARDI

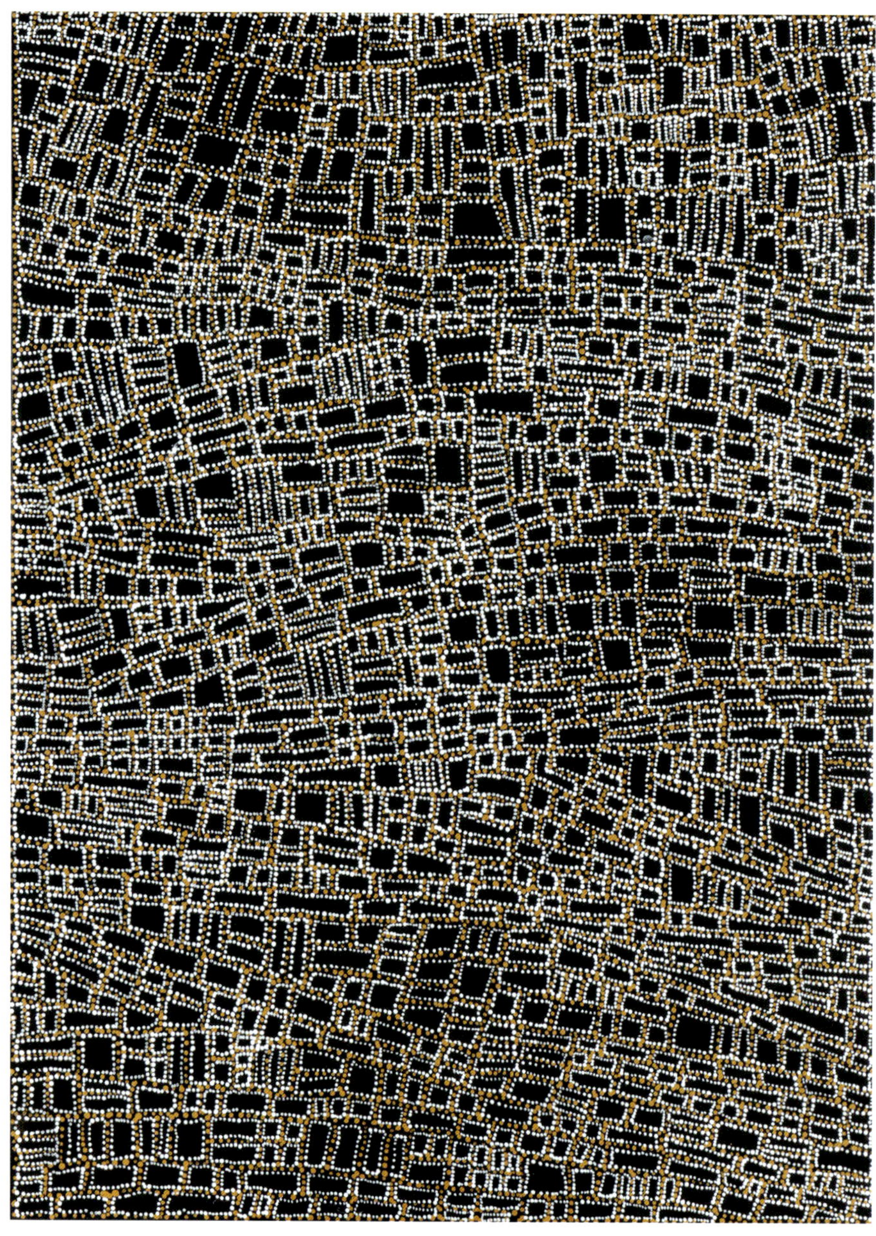

70

Kamtakurlangu Tjukurrpa, 2010

Acrylic on canvas, 120 × 90 cm
Philippson Collection

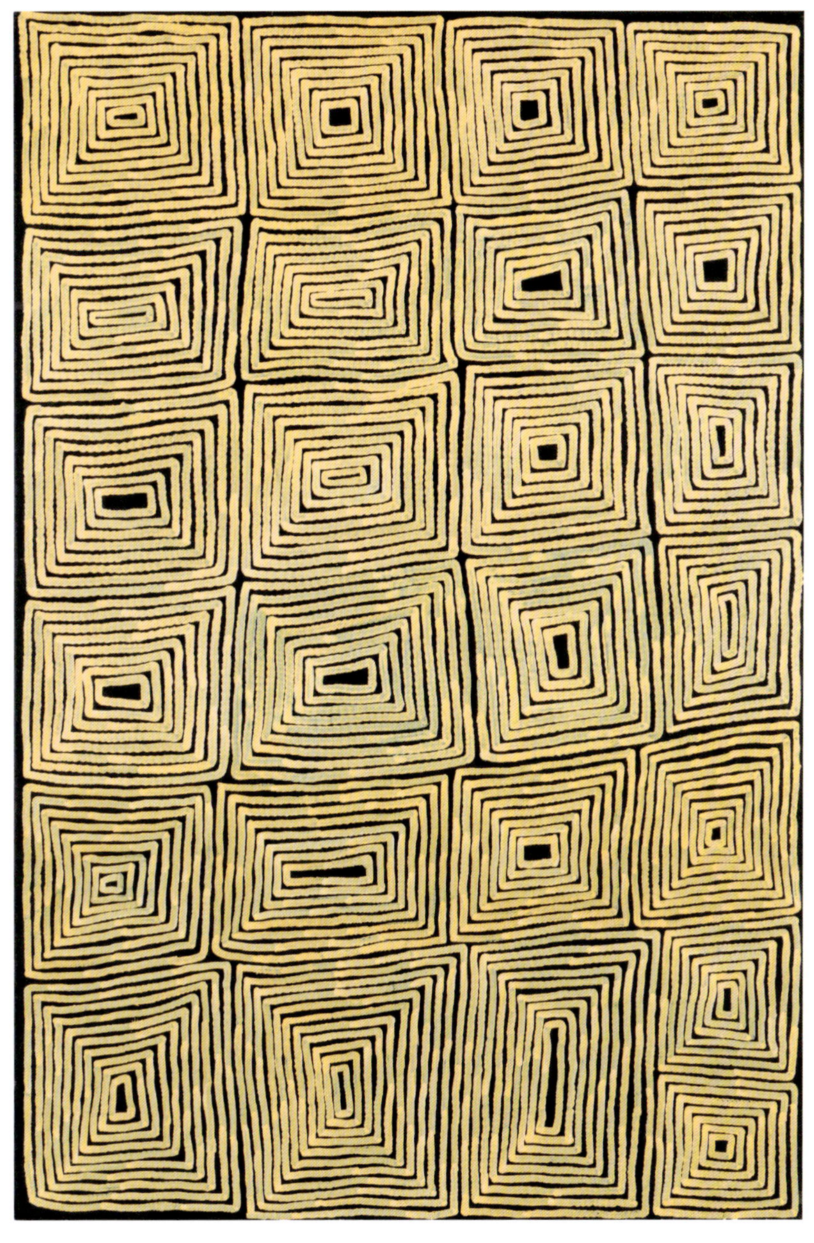

Tingari Ancestors, 2003

Acrylic on canvas, 180 × 120 cm
Philippson Collection

Judy Watson Napangardi (ca. 1925–2016) is a member of the Warlpiri ethnic group. Although she was a small and fragile-looking girl, she quickly proved to have a prodigiously strong character. Thus, she travelled through her family's territories on several occasions, visiting the sites of Mina Mina or Yingipurlangu, between the Gibson and Tanami Deserts. In this harsh environment, she learned the traditional knowledge reflected in her paintings. However, it was not until 1986 that she started painting for the benefit of the Artists Cooperative of Yuendumu. She has retained the Warlpiri's rich palette of bright colours. Like the works produced by the Napangardi clan, her pictures focus on the stories of the Mina Mina site, (where women are the custodians) and the women's ceremonies that keep their memory alive. Her work is instantly recognisable with its distinctive background of large curved arabesques in shimmering colours. Her representation encompasses the full character of the Mina Mina sacred site: vegetation, water, landscape and history all combine harmoniously.

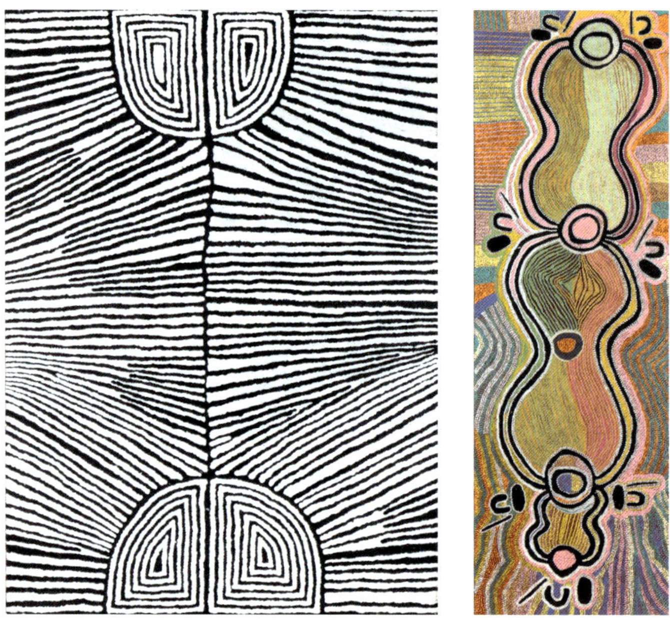

Judy Watson Napangardi – Untitled

Acrylic on canvas, 98 × 73 cm
Philippson Collection

Maggie Watson Napangardi – *Ngalyipi Tjukurrpa*, 1996

Acrylic on canvas, 182 × 61 cm
Philippson Collection

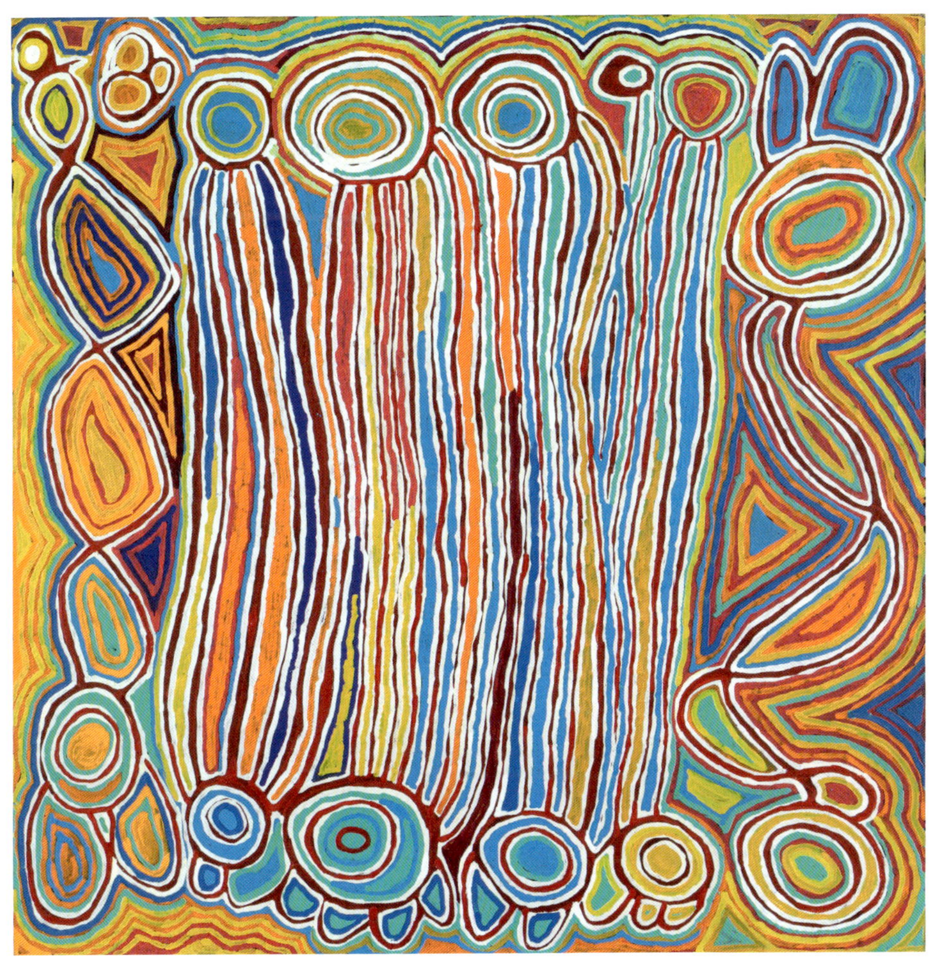

Mina Mina

Acrylic on linen, 120 × 120 cm
Philippson Collection

DAVID MILLER

Born around 1951, David Miller is a Pitjantjatjara man who lives in the remote community settlement of Kanpi in the Western Desert. He spent his early years in the traditional Aparatjara settlement before moving to Inarki. Together with his family, he embarked on long journeys on foot from Warburtin to Ernabella, where he attended ritual ceremonies and the exchange of dingoes to obtain tea and flour. His family continued to roam the Northern Territory to the various cattle stations to find work. At the age of sixteen, the young man found work at Todmorton near Oodnadatta, before moving to Amata where he lived for several years. Eventually, he would return to his original West to be introduced to traditional rituals and take part in setting up the communities. In 2005, he discovered painting during a training programme offered to people living in the Pitjantjatjara communities. In 2008, he made it his main activity. In the artist's own words, *Perentie Track* represents the area where his father was born, somewhere on the track near Perentie Waltijitjara, while his community was being deported to a camp.

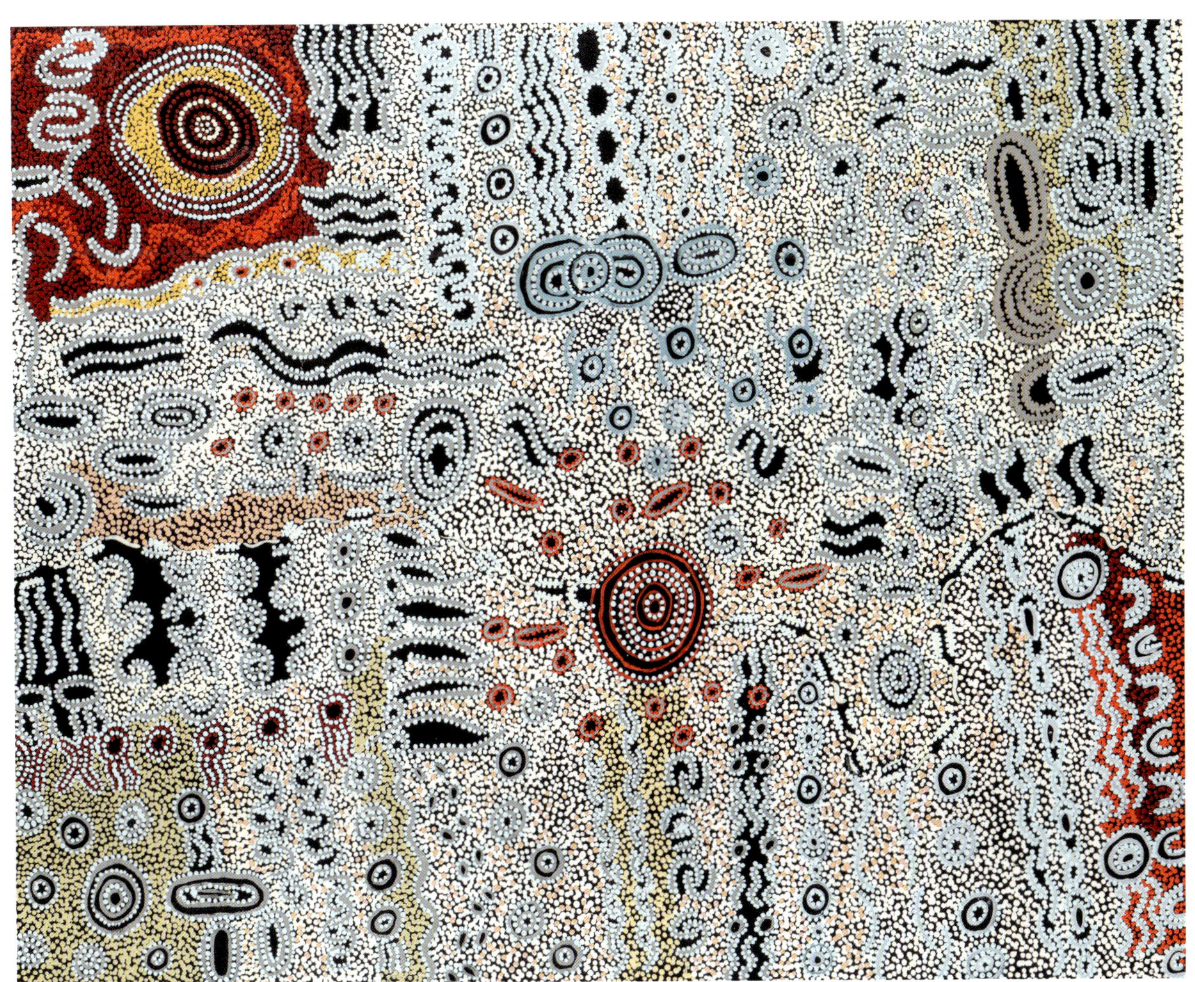

Perenties Track, 2012

Acrylic on linen, 120 × 152 cm
Philippson Collection

Rover Thomas Joolama (1926–1998) was born in Yalda Soak, near Gunawaggi, in the driest part of the Western Desert. Firmly attached to his traditional lifestyle, his father was killed by white men. Taken in by a family member, Rover Thomas then headed for the Kimberley. As a desert man, he would remain a herdsman for the rest of his life. Nevertheless, the tragic events of his youth were to leave a lasting impression on him. In his paintings, he showed the abuse perpetrated against his people as well as the economic hardship he endured, particularly when hundreds of farmworkers were made redundant. Condemned to go into exile, these workers filled the makeshift camps set up on the outskirts of white cities. His style, close to that of Paddy Jaminji (ca. 1917–2010), influenced, among others, Rammey Ramsey (ca. 1935), also from the East Kimberley.

In December 1974, Cyclone Tracy destroyed the city of Darwin, which the Aboriginal people of the Kimberley saw as the heartland of Whitefellas' rule. Generally associated with the Rainbow Serpent Ancestor, cyclones, storms, and other torrential rains are seen by the elders as a message. In their eyes, the Ancestors are thus warning against the loss of cultural references. Rover Thomas understood the lesson. A few months later, he moved to Warmun where he received a dream visit from an aunt who had died after a car accident during Cyclone Tracy. She died on the plane to Perth and her spirit embarked on a journey that would take her through various sacred areas to her home in the east where she witnessed the destruction of Darwin by the Rainbow

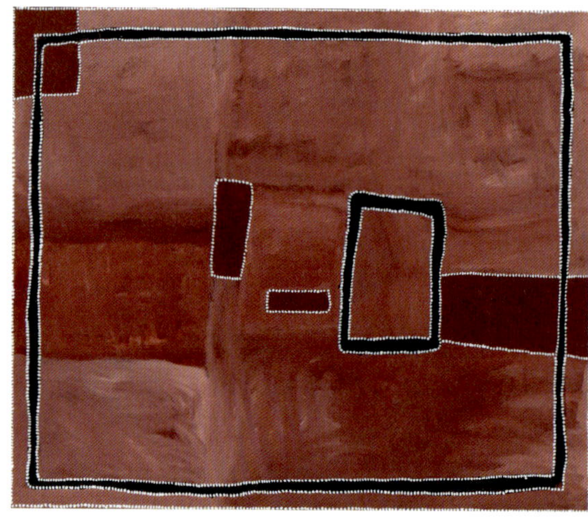

Rammey Ramsey
Warlawoon Country, 2007

Pigment on canvas, 150 × 180 cm
Philippson Collection

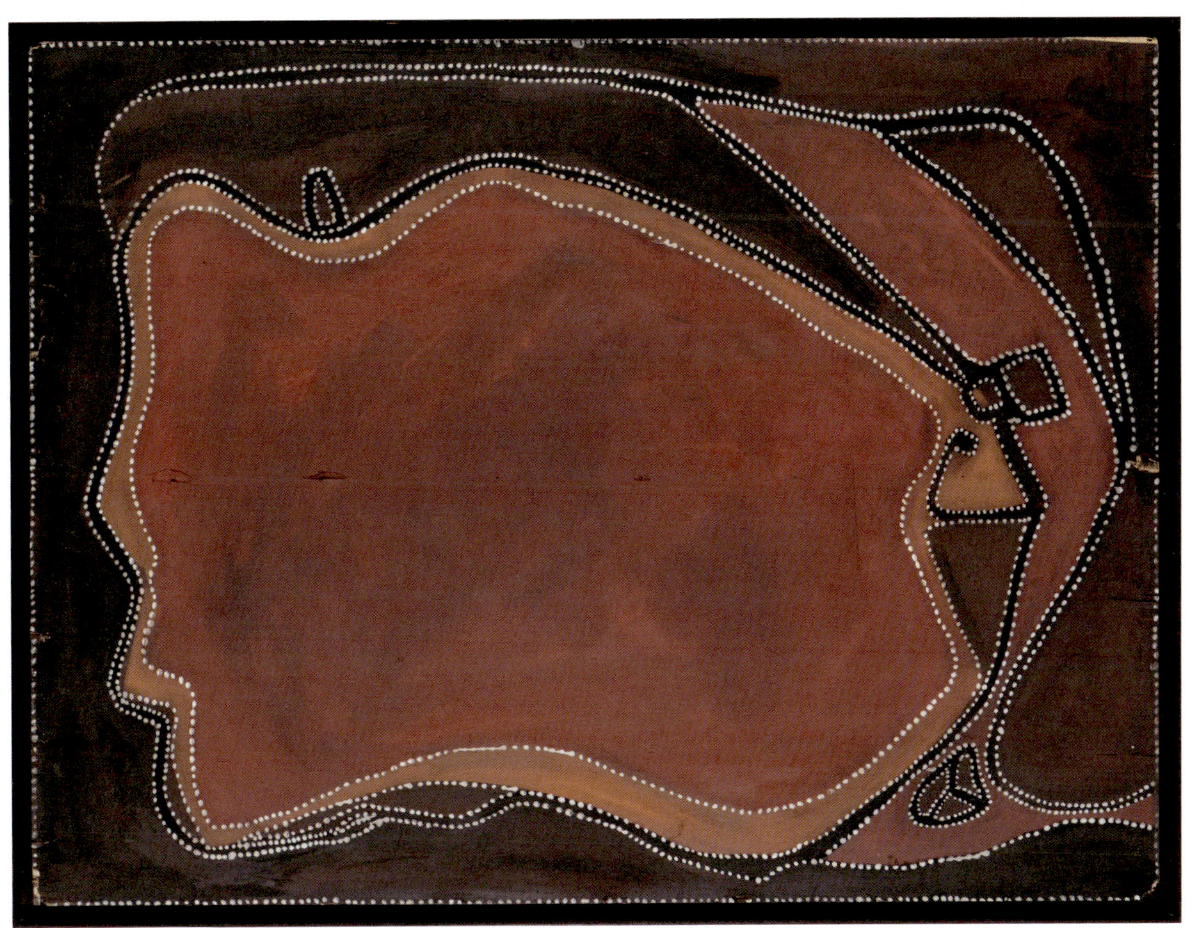

Untitled, 1990

Natural pigment on panel, 113 × 152 cm
Philippson Collection

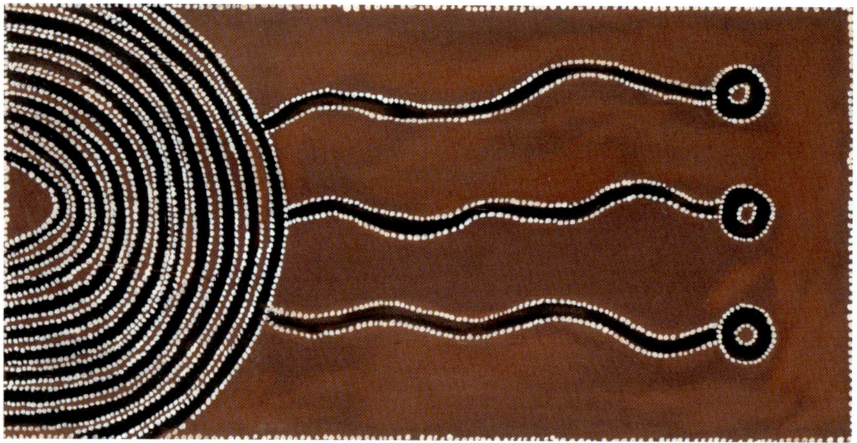

Paddy Jaminji – *Old Tracks to Dreaming Place*, 1979
Natural pigment on panel, 60 × 120 cm
Philippson Collection

Serpent. This story forms the basis of the *Gurirr Gurirr* ceremony that the woman's spirit revealed to Rover Thomas. He became the owner of this ritual, from which he drew his inspiration for his first paintings in 1981. Right from the start, the artist displayed a powerful personal style. To such an extent that the Gija initiates (the oldest members of the Warmun community) were moved to discover such a unique artistic style. They passed on their memories to the painter for him to immortalise them in paintings. An exceptional series is entirely devoted to the exactions and massacres perpetrated by the whites in the 1940s. He depicts the most inhuman tragedies that took place without resorting to overly strong figuration.

In 1995, Rover Thomas returned to his childhood home. In *Bubba Dog Dreaming* — one of a series of works chronicling this journey — the artist shows the site of "Wild Dog Dreaming" in the middle of Yalda Soak. The composition features the rock holes formed by Mother Wild Dog and her puppies. These crevices on the ridges open up into wells interconnected by underground passages. They are associated with the prominent rounded stones typical of the region and constitute vital sources of food for the herds in the very midst of the desert. In the centre of the painting, the "dream" place of the Wild Mother unfolds.

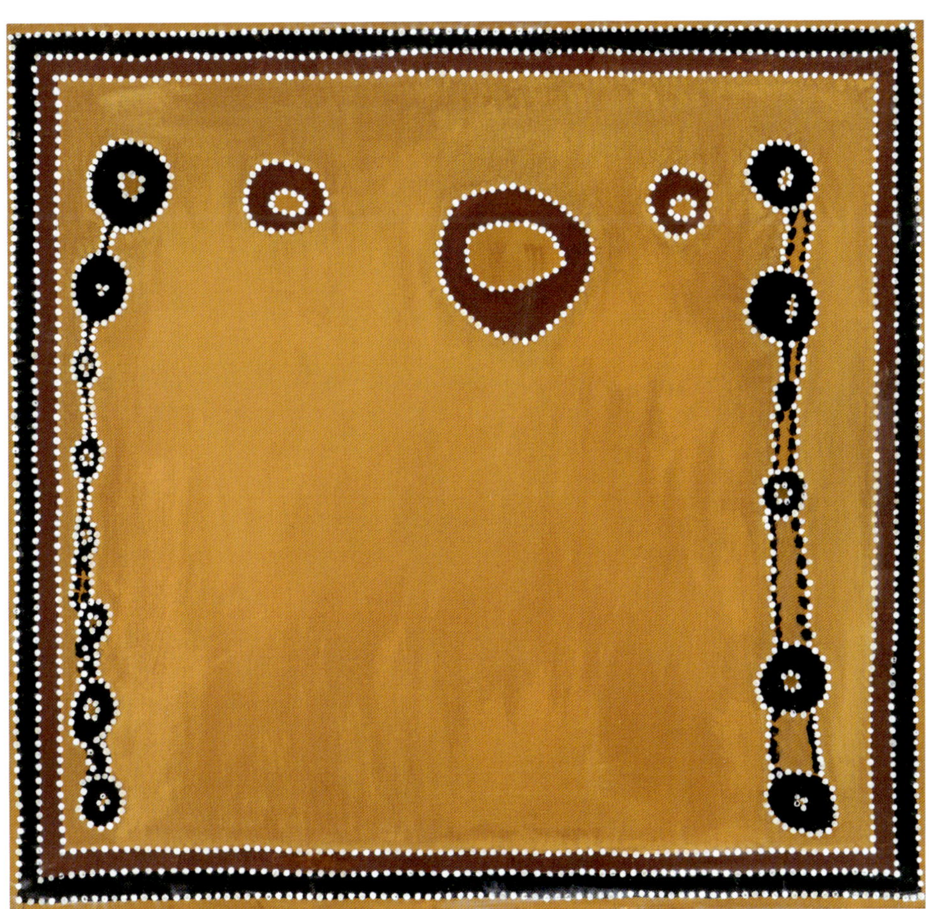

Bubba Dog Dreaming, 1996

Natural pigment on canvas, 98 × 104 cm
Philippson Collection

Born in Riya on the banks of the Turner River, Phyllis Thomas (ca. 1938) grew up in the town before moving to Wyndham and marrying Joe Thomas. The couple then moved to the area and founded the Rugun community, which is linked to the myth of Crocodile Hole. While her husband was involved in the creation of a school, Phyllis endeavoured to teach the fundamental artistic values and techniques of Aboriginal culture there: sculpture, painting, and dance. Crocodile Hole became a major theme in her work, in which she emphasises the richness of both animal and plant life.

In one of her untitled pieces, she beautifully depicts an ecosystem made possible by the quality of the constantly flowing water. The depth of the springs ensures that the water is always fresh. Herds of cattle flock there from all over. The colonists used to fatten their animals there before driving them to the slaughterhouses in Wyndham. Although the artist does not represent the founding events of the "Dreamtime" in this piece, she pays close attention to the landscape with its rivers, waterholes, and pastures that simultaneously form a delicate topography of the site, while evoking its greenery dominated by the baobab tree. His white dotted line, characteristic of the work of other artists based near Warmun, is also found in the compositions of Rusty Peters (1935–2020).

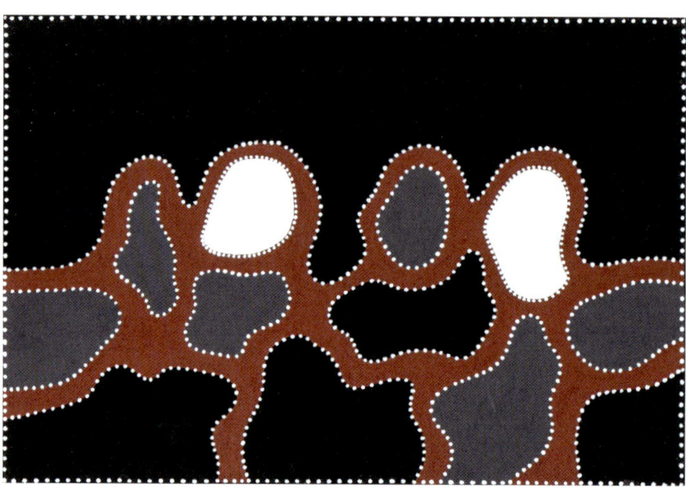

Rusty Peters – *Warrabayan*, 2010

Natural pigment on canvas, 60 × 90 cm
Philippson Collection

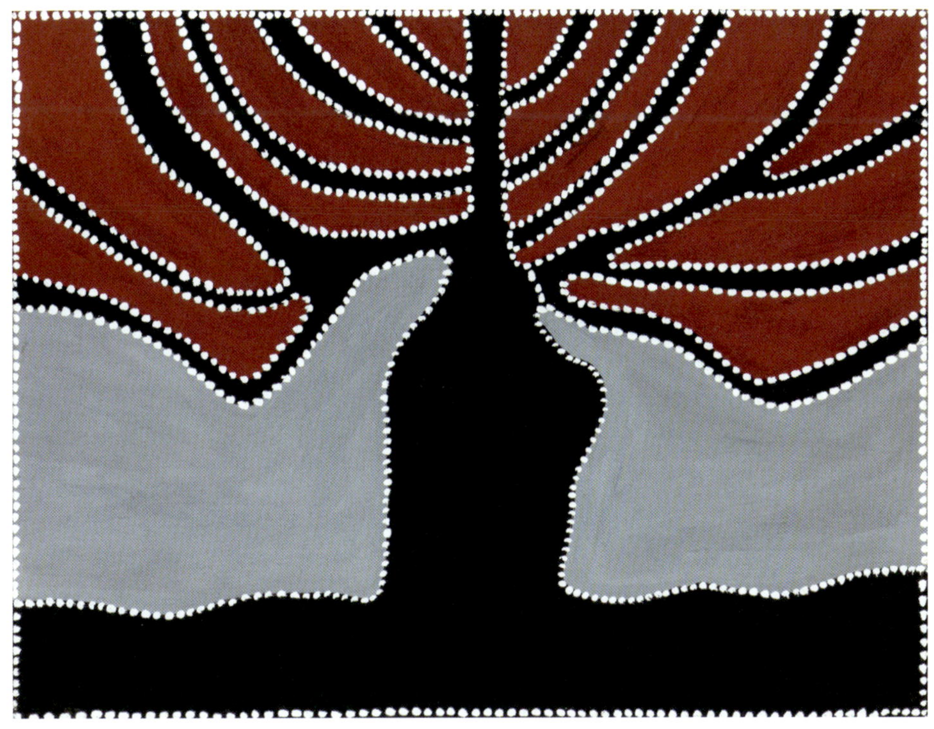

Untitled, 2014

Natural pigment on canvas, 76 × 100 cm
Philippson Collection

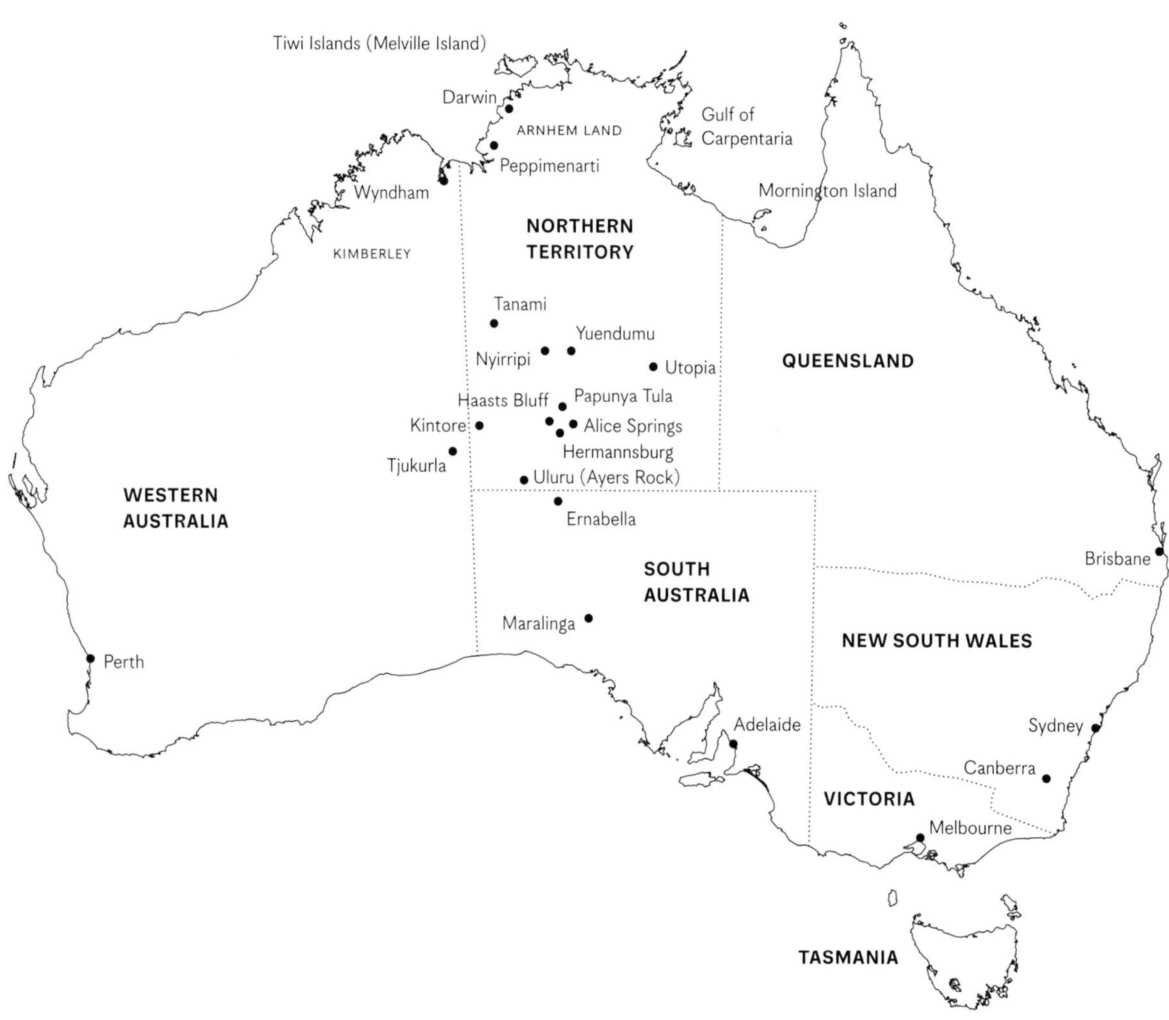
Tiwi Islands (Melville Island)
Darwin
ARNHEM LAND
Gulf of
Carpentaria
Peppimenarti
Wyndham
Mornington Island
NORTHERN
TERRITORY
KIMBERLEY
Tanami
Yuendumu
Nyirripi
Utopia
QUEENSLAND
Haasts Bluff
Papunya Tula
Kintore
Alice Springs
Hermannsburg
Tjukurla
Uluru (Ayers Rock)
WESTERN
AUSTRALIA
Ernabella
SOUTH
AUSTRALIA
Brisbane
Maralinga
NEW SOUTH WALES
Perth
Adelaide
Sydney
Canberra
VICTORIA
Melbourne
TASMANIA

CHRONOLOGY

60,000–50,000 BCE
Arrival of populations from Asia in Australia.

30,000 BCE
First use of ochre in New South Wales graves.

18,000 BCE
First cave paintings in Arnhem Land.

8,000–7,000 BCE
Australia and New Guinea split at the Torres Strait.

7,000 BCE
Development of X-ray style painting in Western Arnhem Land. The internal organs of animals and contents of objects are depicted by transparency.

1606 Under the command of Willem Janszoon, the Dutch ship *Duijfken* reaches the Australian mainland at Cape York.

1623 The crew of Dutch ship Arnhem draws the first map of the coastline of what will later become the north-eastern part of Arnhem Land.

1642 Dutch navigator Abel Tasman maps part of the coast of a territory that he christened Van Diemen's Land, which will later become Tasmania.

1650 First visits of the Makassarese people (today's Sulawesi people in Indonesia) to the northern coast of Australia in search of trepang (sea cucumbers). They establish close ties with the local population up until 1906, when the Australian government puts an end to such relations.

1688 Briton William Dampier enters the King Sound in the Kimberley region on the northwest coast of Australia. He describes the fish traps that he discovers there.

1770 James Cook maps the east coast of Australia, claiming the eastern portion of the Australian continent for King George III, naming it New South Wales.

1788 The fleet of Captain Arthur Phillip establishes the first British penal colony at Sydney Cove. The date of its creation, 26 January, becomes Australia Day.

1790 The Aboriginal population is estimated at one million individuals. Pemulwuy (ca. 1750–1802) is the first Aboriginal Australian to resist colonisation. He wages guerrilla warfare in the Sydney area.

1793 Arrival of the first free settlers.

1800 John Lewin is the first London artist to settle in Australia.

1801–1803 Matthew Flinders explores the Australian coast and discovers the cave paintings on Chasm Island in the Groote Eylandt region. After completing the first tour of Australia, he is first to use the country's current name, which he deemed "more agreeable" than the previously used *Terra Australis*. The name was made official in 1824.

1802 The expedition led by Nicholas Baudin in Tasmania uncovers a hut made of eucalyptus bark whose walls are covered in paintings.

1829 The creation of the Swan River District (West Australia) confirms the full possession of the continent by the British Crown.

1830–1834 The last Tasmanian Aborigines are regrouped and deported to Wybalenna on Flinders Island, in the Bass Strait.

1834 Nyungar massacre in Pinjarra led by Stirling, Governor of the Swan River Colony, and his troops.

1835 Creation of Melbourne.

1835 Batman's Treaty initiates the dispossession of Aboriginal lands in what will become the State of Victoria. The extreme dispersal of Aboriginal groups and their small footprint on their environment prompts settlers to consider the southern continent as *terra nullius*, nobody's land.

1837 George Grey studies the Wandjina paintings. In his opinion, the quality of their craftsmanship could not be attributed to the Aborigines, who were considered to be too primitive. He consequently attributes them to "foreign visitors".

1844–1845 Ludwig Leichhardt leads an expedition enabling him to cross Australia from the bay of what will become Brisbane to Port Essington.

1850 Convicts abandon their settlements. The last deportations are carried out in 1868.

1855 First presentation of bark paintings at the Paris Exposition Universelle.

1872 A telegraph line links Adelaide and Darwin.

1879 Bark paintings from the Northern Territories are presented at the Garden Palace Exhibition in Sydney.

1898 Photographer Charles Kerry takes photographs of the last Bora ceremony in Quambone Station in New South Wales.

1900 Queen Victoria proclaims that Australia's six colonies now form a federation under the name of the Commonwealth of Australia with Melbourne as its capital city.

1912 Employed by Melbourne's National Museum of Victoria, Baldwin Spencer compiles the first collection of Oenpelli's bark paintings.

1913 Founding of the capital of Australia: Canberra.

1914–1918 The sacrifice of some 60,000 Australians during the First World War helps forge a sense of national unity. During the Second World War, 27,000 Australians would die in battle.

1928 Warlpiri massacre at Coniston Station, near Yuendumu, Central Australia.

1929 The first major exhibition of Aboriginal art is presented at the National Museum of Victoria in Melbourne.

1935 A mission is established in Yirrkala, in the East Arnhem Region, Northeast Territory of Australia.

1936 Albert Namatjira produces his first watercolours, embracing Western taste and style. Three years later, a work entitled Haasts Bluff is purchased by the Art Gallery of New South Wales in Sydney.

1943 The *Primitive Art* Exhibition, offering a comprehensive overview of Aboriginal art, is organized in Melbourne at the National Gallery & National Museum of Victoria.

1948 An American-Australian expedition to Arnhem Land brings together collections from Groote Eylandt, Yirrkala, and Oenpelli.

1957 Creation of the Elcho Island Memorial.

1958–1959 Stuart Scougall and Tony Tuckson organise expeditions to the north for the Art Gallery of New South Wales in Sydney. They bring back pukumani poles from Melville Island and the Bathurst Islands as well as bark paintings from Yirrkala.

1963 Aborigines from Yirrkala write a petition on bark in accordance with their cultural traditions, which they present to the House of Representatives in Canberra.

1965 Drawing inspiration from black American movements, freedom marches are organised in New South Wales.

1966 With the introduction of the decimal system, the Australian government produces a new dollar bill with a painting by David Malangi (1927–1999) printed on it. Since Malangi had not been asked for permission, a public debate on appropriation begins.

1967 Following a referendum, the government imposes national legislation concerning Aboriginal people who are counted for the first time in a census. Meanwhile, strikes to demand equal pay for equal work break out.

1971 Following the Yirrkala petition, the local population begin legal action to recuperate their land rights. Although they build a case that profoundly impacts public opinion, they lose the lawsuit.

1971 In the central desert, Geoffrey Bardon encourages a group of elders relegated to the Papunya settlement to paint traditional designs to decorate the walls of the school. They later switch to acrylic on reusable materials such as cardboard, revealing a world based on their initiatory knowledge. This is how Western Desert art begins.

1971 For the very first time, an Aboriginal artist exhibits his bark paintings at the University of Sydney.

1972 A tent is erected in Canberra to serve as an Aboriginal Embassy.

1973 The Australia Council establishes the Aboriginal Arts Board. The first chairman is Dick Roughsey.

1976 Adoption of the Aboriginal Land Rights Act, introducing the movement for the recovery of land rights by Aboriginal communities.

1978 For the first time, two Aborigines receive scholarships to study at Canberra's Australian National University.

1981 Organisation of *Aboriginal Australia*, the first travelling exhibition that broadly reflects the diversity of Aboriginal culture. Aboriginal artists are now featured regularly in the main galleries across the country.

1983 The recognition of Aboriginal art prompts the creation of a department within Canberra's New Australia Art Gallery.

1983 Opening of the first lawsuit for cultural appropriation brought by Yanggarriny Wunungmurra v. the Peter Stripes Fabric. The artist's claims are recognised.

1984 Creation of the National Aboriginal Art Award at Darwin's Museum and Art Gallery of the Northern Territory.

1985 The sacred site of Uluru (Ayers Rock) is returned to its Aboriginal owners.

1986 The South Australian Museum presents *Art and Land*, an exhibition of toas that sheds light on the artistic value of Aboriginal creations for the first time.

1988-1989 *Dreamings: The Art of Aboriginal Australia* travelling exhibition is presented at New York's Asian Center before being shown in Chicago, Los Angeles, Melbourne, and Adelaide. The international acknowledgement of Aboriginal creation — and more specifically of Western Desert artists — begins.

1988 Installation of the Aboriginal Memorial to mark the bicentenary of British colonisation: two hundred hollow log coffins are shown at Canberra's National Gallery of Australia. Michael Nelson Tjakamarra creates a 196-square-metre mosaic for the forecourt of Canberra's New Parliament House, where the Barunga Statement is presented on traditionally painted bark.

1988 Clifford Possum Tjapaltjarri exhibits his paintings at London's ICA. This is the first exhibition of an Aboriginal artist outside Australia.

1989 In Paris, Jean-Hubert Martin incorporates Aboriginal art into his *Magiciens de la Terre* (Magicians of the World). A Yuendumu sand carpet featuring ritual figures interacts with one of Richard Long's circles.

1990 Rover Thomas and Trevor Nickolls are the first Aboriginal artists to represent Australia at the Venice Biennale. They are followed in 1997 by a trio of women: Emily Kame Kngwarreye, Yvonne Koolmatrie, and Judy Watson.

1992 The Mabo Decision gives Aboriginal people the right to their land for the first time. The concept of *terra nullius* is definitively revoked.

1993–1994 For the first time in Europe, the exhibition *Aratjara: Art of the First Australians* presents a broad picture of Aboriginal culture, travelling from Düsseldorf via London to Copenhagen.

2000 The 2000 Summer Olympics in Sydney bring the plight of Australia's Aborigines to the international forefront.

2008 In Parliament, Australian Prime Minister Kevin Rudd offers a national apology to the Stolen Generations for the ill treatment suffered by Aborigines.

2010 Thirteen spaces dedicated to Australian Aboriginal artists and artists from Torres Strait Island are opened at Canberra's National Gallery. This is the largest collection dedicated to Aborigines.

2012–2013 The Quai Branly Museum in Paris presents the exhibition entitled *Aux sources de la Peinture Aborigène – Australie Tjukurrtjanu*.

2013 The Royal Academy of Arts, London organises a large-scale exhibition entitled *Australia*, which presents a complete overview of the nation's first two centuries of artistic production.

FROM ASSIMILATION TO RECOGNITION

Assimilation — Australian governments long espoused a deliberate policy to force Aborigines to adopt the lifestyle of the dominant European Australian majority. In their minds, the Aborigines were no different to the successive generations of Asian immigrants who settled in the major Australian cities and adopted the "local" way of life. This assimilation policy came with a determination to marginalise Aboriginal traditions, or even to prohibit their practice. The removal of Aboriginal children and forced internment in institutions where assimilation was imposed on them was also justified in the name of this policy. In the 1970s, as public awareness of the Aboriginal "problem" gained momentum, the assimilationist obsession gave way to a policy of empowerment of indigenous peoples.

Outstation Movement — The strategy to concentrate aboriginal groups in government facilities and missions initially led to a profound crisis. A reverse movement ensued, inviting Aboriginal groups to re-locate according to their identities and in places that were more in touch with their ancestral traditions. As a result, small communities settled and grew on their traditional lands.

Land rights — In the 1960s, the question of land rights became central to the struggle of Aboriginal communities for the recognition of their legal existence. Until 1967, in accordance with the principle of *terra nullius* that had governed colonisation, the Aborigines were not considered to be citizens and consequently had no rights to land. Led in the Northern Territories, this struggle resulted in the *Aboriginal Land Rights Act*, which restored the rights of the northern and central communities. However, their relationship to the land remains all the more complicated because the Dreamtime makes the entire landscape sacred. In contrast, the protection of Aboriginal heritage is still not assured. The media regularly reports on the destruction of archaeological sites for economic and industrial purposes.

Property — The concept of personal ownership is unknown to the Aborigines. Property can only be communal and also covers the reproduction of ritually designed patterns. This explains the ambiguity surrounding the sale of works of art to institutions or private individuals. These works are then not allowed to be exhibited by the communities for reasons that can be described as spiritual, if not religious.

AFTERWORD

To give you a better understanding of the *Aboriginalities* exhibition, we would like to provide some context for presenting Aboriginal art.

Showing Aboriginal painting is no easy task. After centuries of alienation, this ancestral artistic practice is today recognised and protected. Aboriginal creation cannot be compared to Western genres: its anthropological roots in the "Dreamtime" confer a sacred dimension that cannot be revealed to everyone.

Following a request from the Australian Embassy, we have decided not to exhibit the beautiful "tjurungas" (or "churingas") from the Africa Museum in Tervueren. This characteristic object of the Aboriginal peoples of central Australia is owned by a group, or an individual who receives it based on its totemic origin and the location where it was conceived by the spirit of their Ancestor. The "tjurunga" is presented at the end of an initiatory ceremony involving rituals and songs, emphasising its sacred value. This present is regarded as a gift from an Ancestor and therefore constitutes a link to the "Dreamtime."

Contemporary Aboriginal painting draws largely from this same initiatory knowledge. Since 2009, the *Indigenous Art Code* has implemented rules to ensure respect for traditions and cultural interdictions in the production and marketing of this art. Art centres and other cooperatives that supervise and commercialise the productions of indigenous artists from the southern continent conform to this code to ensure that the market is equitable and respectful of the artists and their traditions.

Relayed by governmental authorities in Australia and throughout the world, the *Indigenous Art Code* aims to impose its status as the exclusive criterion for the recognition of Aboriginal art. In Australia, this construction of the market into a monopoly of art centres has provoked much debate and consequently, membership of the circle formed by the Indigenous Art Code is now open to private galleries. To be eligible, these galleries must provide answers to a number of questions that we also support, in order to ascertain the integrity and transparency of the relationship between galleries and artists:

- How has the artist or art centre that submitted the work been paid, and is the sum fair?
- Has the indigenous artist been informed as to the terms of sale of their work?
- Does a written contract outline the terms of the agreement and in what form?
- Have the sale and payment been recorded and catalogued in a manner that clearly determines the nature and identity of the work sold and does this information remain accessible to the artist?

While some may interpret these questions as a desire for national control, many others believe that they are key in protecting the authenticity of Aboriginal art, which has been defended by generations of anthropologists.

In partnership with collectors, the Royal Museums have been very careful to check how the works being exhibited were originally introduced on the Australian market and then, through the successive sales that shape the life of an artwork, the terms of their arrival on the Western art scene.

WORKS SHOWN IN THE EXHIBITION

Cat. 1

TERESA STEVENS
Nyapati Tjukurrpa, 2018

Acrylic on canvas, 151 × 100 cm
Philippson Collection, inv. TS1

Cat. 2 (p. 27)

GABRIELLA POSSUM NUNGURRAYI (ca. 1967)
My Country

Acrylic on canvas, 80 × 100 cm
Philippson Collection, inv. GPN2b

Cat. 3 (p. 25)

GABRIELLA POSSUM NUNGURRAYI (ca. 1967)
Grand Mother Country, 2015

Acrylic on canvas, 80 × 100 cm
Philippson Collection, inv. GPN2a

Cat. 4

VICTOR MAGARIÑOS D. (1924–1993)
Bandas magneticas, 1959

Felt-tipped pen on paper, 312 × 257 mm
RMFAB, donated by the artist, 1986,
inv. 10578

Cat. 5

VICTOR MAGARIÑOS D. (1924–1993)
Nucleo, 1965

Felt-tipped pen on paper, 257 × 317 mm
RMFAB, donated by the artist, 1986,
inv. 10580

Cat. 6

VICTOR MAGARIÑOS D. (1924–1993)
Bocetos. Pintura cosmologica, 1983

Felt-tipped pen on paper, 221 × 340 mm
RMFAB, donated by the artist, 1986,
inv. 10584

Cat. 7 (p. 36)

TJAWINA PORTER NAMPITJINPA (ca. 1950)
Punkilpirri, 2009

Acrylic on canvas, 122 × 91 cm
Philippson Collection, inv. TPN1

Cat. 8 (p. 38)

MAISIE CAMPBELL NAPALTJARRI (ca. 1958)
Kapi Tjukurrpa & Women Ceremonies, 2011

Acrylic on canvas, 152 × 152 cm
Philippson Collection, inv. MCN1

Cat. 9 (p. 38)

MAISIE CAMPBELL NAPALTJARRI (ca. 1958)
Kapi Tjukurrpa, Minyma Inmaku, 2011

Acrylic on canvas, 152 × 183 cm
Philippson Collection, inv. MCN2

Cat. 10 (p. 39)

MAISIE CAMPBELL NAPALTJARRI (ca. 1958)
Kapi Tjukurrpa, 2010

Acrylic on Belgian linen, 122 × 91 cm
Philippson Collection, inv. MCN3

Cat. 11 (p. 37)

TJAWINA PORTER NAMPITJINPA (ca. 1950)
Tjalili, 2009

Acrylic on linen, 181 × 305 cm
RMFAB, donated by Yanda Aboriginal Art,
Alice Springs (Australia), 2020, inv. 12599

Cat. 12

RICHARD LONG (ca. 1945)
Utah Circle, [1989]

Stones from Utah (United States), ø 600 cm
RMFAB, acquired in 1991, inv. 11335

Cat. 13 (p. 50)

SALLY GABORI (1924–2015)
Big Crocodile, 2005

Acrylic on canvas, 91 × 210 cm
Philippson Collection, inv. SG2

Cat. 14

KUDDITJI KNGWARREYE (ca. 1928–2017)
My Country

Acrylic on canvas, 60 × 60 cm
Philippson Collection, inv. KK3

Cat. 15 (p. 54)

KUDDITJI KNGWARREYE (ca. 1928–2017)
My Country, 2013

Acrylic on canvas, 60 × 60 cm
Philippson Collection, inv. KK2

Cat. 16

JOSIE KUNOTH PETYARRE (ca. 1959)
Untitled, 2015

Acrylic on linen, 80 × 60 cm
Philippson Collection, inv. JKP2

Cat. 17 (p. 61)

JOSIE KUNOTH PETYARRE (ca. 1959)
Sugar Bag, 2018

Acrylic on linen, 150 × 350 cm
Philippson Collection, inv. JKP5

Cat. 18

IVAN NAMIRRKKI (ca. 1961)
Ginga-Fresh Water Crocodile at Mambulugarri, 1989

Pigment on wood bark
Philippson Collection, inv. IN1

Cat. 19 (p. 47)

TIMOTHY WULANJBIRR (ca. 1969)
Ngalyod the Rainbow Serpent, 2001

Natural pigment on eucalyptus bark, 83 × 54 cm
Philippson Collection, inv. TW1

Cat. 20 (p. 78)

PADDY JAMINJI (ca. 1912–1996)
Old Tracks to Dreaming Place, 1979

Natural pigment on panel, 60 × 120 cm
Philippson Collection, inv. PJ1

Cat. 21 (p. 49)

MARIKA DHUWARRWARR (ca. 1946)
Yalanbara-Larrakitji (hollow log), 2020

Natural pigment on Acacia, 219 × 20 cm
Philippson Collection, inv. MD1

Cat. 22 (p. 49)

TIMOTHY COOK MARNTUPUNI (ca. 1958)
Untitled (Tutini and Tunga), 2007

Natural pigment on ironwood, height: 260 cm
Philippson Collection, inv. TCM1

Cat. 23 (p. 49)

Malaluba Gumana (1952–2020)
Garrimala, 2007

Natural pigment on Acacia, height: 186 cm
Philippson Collection, inv. MGU1

Cat. 24

ANDRÉ WILLEQUET (1921–1998)
Love Column, [1972]

Polychrome lime wood , 239 × 40,5 × 37,2 cm
RMFAB, donated by the artist, 1982, inv. 9581

Cat. 25 (p. 12)

LINDA SYDDICK NAPALTJARRI (ca. 1937)
Kangoroo Man Story, 2014

Acrylic on canvas, 78 × 103 cm
Philippson Collection, inv. LSN1

Cat. 26 (p. 16)

SHORTY LUNGKARDA TJUNGURRAYI (ca. 1920–1987)
Death Story, 1972

Acrylic on canvas, 36 × 23 cm
Philippson Collection, inv. SLT1

Cat. 27 (p. 11)

JOHNNY WARANGKULA TJUPURRULA (ca. 1918–2001)
Dingo Camp at Tinki, 1973

Acrylic on canvas, 79 × 61 cm
Philippson Collection, inv. JWT1

Cat. 28 (p. 13)

KAAPA MBITJANA TJAMPITJINPA (ca. 1920–1989)
Yala at Yantjupu, 1973

Acrylic on canvas, 55 × 37 cm
Philippson Collection, inv. KT1

Cat. 29

BELINDA NAPANGARDI
Minyma (Women's) Dreaming, 1981

Acrylic on wood, 72 × 13,5 cm
Philippson Collection, inv. BN1

Cat. 30

ANAWARI MITCHELL (ca. 1959)
Kuriala Seven Sisters Place, 2014

Acrylic on linen, 92 × 92 cm
Philippson Collection, inv. AM1

Cat. 31

PEGGY ROCKMAN NAPALJARRI (ca. 1940)
Warna Jukurrpa (Snake Dreaming), 1988

Acrylic on linen
Philippson Collection, inv. PRN

Cat. 32 (p. 7)

NAATA NUNGURRAYI (ca. 1932)
Marrapinti, 2005

Acrylic on canvas, 182 × 152 cm
Philippson Collection, inv. NAAN2

Cat. 33

LOUIE COWBOY PWERLE (ca. 1941)
Ngookwala Cave, 1992

Acrylic on canvas, 212 × 122 cm
Philippson Collection, inv. LCP2

Cat. 34

MINNIE NAPANANGKA
Walabi Dreaming, 1992

Acrylic on canvas
Philippson Collection, inv. MN3

Cat. 35 (p. 20)

CLIFFORD POSSUM TJAPALTJARRI (1932–2002)
Untitled, 2001

Acrylic on canvas, 92 × 151 cm
Philippson Collection, inv. CPT2

Cat. 36 (p. 43)

JONATHAN KUMINTJARRA BROWN (1960–1997)
Broad Shield Design, 1995

Ochre on linen, 193 × 101 cm
Philippson Collection, inv. JKB1

Cat. 37 (p. 75)

DAVID MILLER (ca. 1951)
Perenties Track, 2012

Acrylic on linen, 120 × 152 cm
Philippson Collection, inv. DM1

Cat. 38

WALANGKURA TJAPALTJARRI
Untitled

Acrylic on canvas, 122 × 152 cm
Philippson Collection, inv. WGKT1

Cat. 39 (p. 29)

THOMAS TJAPALTJARRI (ca. 1964)
Tingari, 2010

Acrylic on canvas, 122 × 152 cm
Philippson Collection, inv. TT2

Cat. 40 (p. 31)

WALALA TJAPALTJARRI (ca. 1970)
Tingari, 2014

Acrylic on canvas, 122 × 152 cm
Philippson Collection, inv. WT4

Cat. 41

GEORGE WARD TJUNGURRAYI (ca. 1945)
Tingari Cycle, 2007

Acrylic on canvas, 112 × 152 cm
Philippson Collection, inv. GWT3

Cat. 42

JEAN DUBUFFET (1901–1985)
The Destroyed Castle, 1952

Oil on canvas, 130 × 162 cm
RMFAB, acquired in 1954, inv. 6713

Cat. 43 (p. 45)

JONATHAN KUMINTJARRA BROWN (1960–1997)
Maralinga – Dead Emus, 1992

Pigment, emu feathers on panel, 71 × 92 cm
Philippson Collection, inv. JKB2

Cat. 44 (p. 15)

CHARLIE TAWARA TJUNGURRAYI (ca. 1921–1999)
Untitled (Emu Dreaming), 1975

Acrylic on canvas, 76 × 60 cm
Philippson Collection, inv. CTT1

Cat. 45

JANET LONG NAKAMARRA (ca. 1960)
Frog Dreaming

Acrylic on canvas, 111 × 122 cm
Philippson Collection, inv. JLN1

Cat. 46

JOHN LEWIS TJAPANGATI (ca.1955)
Kapi Tjukurrpa Mina Mina [Water Dreams], 2011

Acrylic on canvas, 101 × 111 cm
Philippson Collection, inv. JLT3

Cat. 47

NGIPI WARD (1949–2014)
Kapitu-Kapitu, 2011

Acrylic on canvas, 100 × 100 cm
Philippson Collection, inv. NW1

Cat. 48 (p. 72)

MAGGIE WATSON NAPANGARDI (ca. 1921–2004)
Ngalyipi Tjukurrpa, 1996

Acrylic on canvas, 182 × 61 cm
Philippson Collection, inv. MWN2

Cat. 49

MAGGIE WATSON NAPANGARDI (ca. 1921–2004)
Digging Sticks, 1990

Acrylic on canvas, 76 × 91 cm
Philippson Collection, inv. MWN1

Cat. 50 (p. 73)

JUDY WATSON NAPANGARDI (ca. 1925–2016)
Mina Mina

Acrylic on linen, 120 × 120 cm
Philippson Collection, inv. JWN3

Cat. 51

PADDY JAPALJARRI SIMS (ca. 1917–2010)
Witi Jukurrpa (Ceremonial Poles), 1999

Acrylic on linen
Philippson Collection, inv. PJS

Cat. 52 (p. 41)

BILL WHISKEY TJAPALTJARRI (ca. 1920–2008)
Rockholes and Country near the Olgas, 2008

Acrylic on linen, 153 × 154 cm
Philippson Collection, inv. BWT1

Cat. 53

SERGE VANDERCAM (1924–2005)
The Hanged Man, 1962

Oil on canvas, 149 × 140 cm
RMFAB, acquired in 1962, inv. 6965

Cat. 54 (p. 21)

CLIFFORD POSSUM TJAPALTJARRI (1932–2002)
Rock Wallaby Dreaming, 1986

Acrylic on canvas, 127 × 162 cm
Philippson Collection, inv. CPT3

Cat. 55 (p. 17)

DON TJUNGURRAYI (ca. 1938)
Men's Corroboree, 1993

Acrylic on linen, 118 × 190 cm
Philippson Collection, inv. DT2

Cat. 56

WILLIAM SANDY (ca. 1944)
Untitled, ca. 1990

Acrylic on canvas, 122 × 91 cm
Philippson Collection, inv. WS1

Cat. 57 (p. 23)

CLIFFORD POSSUM TJAPALTJARRI (1932–2002)
Walk Around Woman at Napperby, 1995

Acrylic on canvas, 125 × 75 cm
Philippson Collection, inv. CPT1

Cat. 58

DON TJUNGURRAYI (ca. 1938)
Untitled

Acrylic on linen, 102 × 112 cm
Philippson Collection, inv. DT1

Cat. 59 (p. 35)

CHARLIE TJAPANGATI (ca. 1949)
Tingari Cycle

Acrylic on canvas, 122 × 92 cm
Philippson Collection, inv. CT1

Cat. 60 (p. 54)

EMILY KAME KNGWARREYE (1910–1996)
Body Paint, 1995

Acrylic on paper, 76 × 51 cm
Philippson Collection, inv. EKK3

Cat. 61

CORNELIA TIPUAMANTUMIRRI TJAKAMARRA (ca. 1930)
Waves, 2014

Acrylic on canvas, 80 × 150 cm
Philippson Collection, inv. COT1

Cat. 62

KITTY KANTILLA (1928–2003)
Parlini Jilammmara, 1996

Natural pigment on paper, 101 × 118 cm
Philippson Collection, inv. KKKP2

Cat. 63

JOHN LEWIS TJAPANGATI (ca. 1955)
Body Scarification, 2011

Acrylic on canvas, 122 × 152 cm
Philippson Collection, inv. JLT4

Cat. 64

JOHN LEWIS TJAPANGATI (ca. 1955)
Body Scarification, 2012

Acrylic on canvas, 152 × 46 cm
Philippson Collection, inv. JLT1

Cat. 65

ABIE JANGALA (1919–2002)
Ngapa Water, 1997

Acrylic on linen, 91 × 91 cm
Philippson Collection, inv. AJ1

Cat. 66

EMILY KAME KNGWARREYE (ca. 1910–1996)
Emily's Country, 1994

Acrylic on linen, 89 × 121 cm
Philippson Collection, inv. EKK4

Cat. 67 (p. 55)

EMILY KAME KNGWARREYE (ca. 1910–1996)
Anooralya Yam Awelye, 1994

Acrylic on linen, 70 × 90 cm
Philippson Collection, inv. EKK2

Cat. 68

EMILY KAME KNGWARREYE (ca. 1910–1996)
Pencyl Yam Dreaming, 1995

Acrylic on linen, 60 × 90 cm
Philippson Collection, inv. EKK1

Cat. 69

Thruster

Wood, colouring, carving, red pigment, white pigment, plant fiber, plant material (?), 74.5 × 13.5 × 2.5 cm
Tervuren, Royal Museum for Central Africa, inv. EO.1968.32.4

Cat. 70

Boomerang

Wood, colouring, 51 × 5 × 1.5 cm
Tervuren, Royal Museum for Central Africa, inv. EO.1967.63.5486

Cat. 71

Boomerang

Wood, colouring, 56 × 6 × 1 cm
Tervuren, Royal Museum for Central Africa, inv. EO.1980.1.14

Cat. 72

Boomerang

Wood, colouring, white pigment, 63.5 × 7.5 × 1.5 cm
Tervuren, Royal Museum for Central Africa, inv. EO.1979.1.1531

Cat. 73

Pendant

Shell, carving, reddish-brown pigment, 22 × 4.5 × 1 cm
Tervuren, Royal Museum for Central Africa, inv. EO.1979.1.1534

Cat. 74 (p. 33)

WARLIMPIRRNGA TJAPALTJARRI (ca. 1950)
Tingari, 2015

Acrylic on paper, 91 × 122 cm
Philippson Collection, inv. WPAT2

Cat. 75

DEBRA MC DONALD NANGALA (ca. 1963)
Sand Hills – Tali Tjuta, 2010

Acrylic on canvas, 61 × 128 cm
Philippson Collection, inv. DDMDN1

Cat. 76

SOL LEWITT (1928-2007)
Yellow & Red, Black & Blue, 1972

Coloured India ink, pen on paper, 358 × 278 mm
RMFAB, acquired in 1990, inv. 11292

Cat. 77 (p. 18)

GEORGE TJUNGURRAYI (ca. 1947)
Mamultjulkunga, 2004

Acrylic on canvas, 76 × 91 cm
Philippson Collection, inv. GT1

Cat. 78

Shield

Wood, carving, red and white pigment, 64.5 × 9.5 × 5.5 cm
Tervuren, Royal Museum for Central Africa, inv. EO.1969.34.3

Cat. 79

Shield

Wood, brown, black and green pigment, 88.5 × 37 × 10 cm
Tervuren, Royal Museum for Central Africa, inv. EO.1968.12.1

Cat. 80

Shield

Wood, carving, red and white pigment, 80.5 × 12 × 5 cm
Tervuren, Royal Museum for Central Africa, inv. EO. 1969.34.2

Cat. 81

Shield

Wood, carving, red and brown (?) pigment, 103.5 × 21 × 6.5 cm
Tervuren, Royal Museum for Central Africa, inv. EO.1964.48.127

Cat. 82 (pp. 66–67)

DEBBIE BROWN NAPALTJARRI (ca. 1985)
Tali Tjuta (Many Sand Hills), 2019

Acrylic on linen, 244 × 485 cm
RMFAB, donated by Yanda Aboriginal Art, Alice Springs (Australia), 2020, inv. 12597

Cat. 83

KITTY KANTILLA (1928–2003)
Untitled, 1994

Natural pigment on paper, 57 × 38 cm
Philippson Collection, inv. KKKP1

Cat. 84

BARNEY CAMPBELL TJAKAMARRA (ca. 1928–2006)
Malliera, 2003

Acrylic on canvas, 137 × 191 cm
Philippson Collection, inv. BCT2

Cat. 85 (p. 19)

GEORGE TJUNGURRAYI (ca. 1947)
Mamultjulkunga, 2004

Acrylic on canvas, 152 × 182 cm
Philippson Collection, inv. GT2

Cat. 86

TOMMY WATSON YANNIMA (ca. 1935–2017)
Untitled, 2014

Acrylic on canvas, 120 × 180 cm
Philippson Collection, inv. YTW1

Cat. 87

SALLY GABORI (1924–2015)
Story Place, My Father's Country, 2005

Acrylic on canvas, 76 × 101 cm
Philippson Collection, inv. SG1

Cat. 88

KATARA BUTLER NAPALTJARRI (ca. 1946)
Rock Holes at Warlukantjina, 2016

Acrylic on linen, 152 × 152 cm
Philippson Collection, inv. KB1

Cat. 89 (p. 57)

MINNIE PWERLE (1915–2006)
Bush Melon

Acrylic on canvas, 180 × 120 cm
Philippson Collection, inv. MP2

Cat. 90

SALLY GABORI (1924–2015)
Dibirdibi Country, 2012

Acrylic on canvas, 196 × 111 cm
Philippson Collection, inv. SG4

Cat. 91

LOUIS VAN LINT (1909–1986)
Autumnal Wildness, 1960

Oil on canvas, 200 × 151.5 cm
RMFAB, acquired in 1961, inv. 6917

Cat. 92 (p. 71)

RONNIE TJAMPITJINPA (ca. 1943)
Tingari Ancestors, 2003

Acrylic on canvas, 180 × 120 cm
Philippson Collection, inv. RT3

Cat. 93

BARNEY CAMPBELL TJAKAMARRA (ca. 1928–2006)
Tingari Cycle

Acrylic on canvas, 122 × 91 cm
Philippson Collection, inv. BCT1

Cat. 94

WARLIMPIRRNGA TJAPALTJARRI (ca. 1950)
Tingari, 2015

Acrylic on paper, 122 × 152 cm
Philippson Collection, inv. WPAT1

Cat. 95 (pp. 8, 68–69)

MARY BROWN NAPANGARDI (ca. 1953)
Women's Ceremony, 2019

Acrylic on linen, 244 × 485 cm
RMFAB, donated by Yanda Aboriginal Art, Alice Springs (Australia), 2020, inv. 12598

Cat. 96 (p. 14)

WILLY TJUNGURRAYI (ca. 1932–2018)
Untitled – Tali Tjuta, 2004

Acrylic on Belgian linen, 111 × 102 cm
Philippson Collection, inv. WYT1

Cat. 97 (p. 88)

GEORGE WARD TJUNGURRAYI (ca. 1945)
Tingari Cycle, 2009

Acrylic on canvas, 200 × 203 cm
Philippson Collection, inv. GWT2

Cat. 98 (p. 70)

DOROTHY NAPANGARDI (ca. 1950–2013)
Kamtakurlangu Tjukurrpa, 2010

Acrylic on canvas, 120 × 90 cm
Philippson Collection, inv. DN2

Cat. 99

JOAN WUMALI NAGOMARA
Nurududu, 2008

Acrylic on linen, 80 × 120 cm
Philippson Collection, inv. JWN1

Cat. 100

ELIZABETH NYUMI NUNGURRAYI (ca. 1947)
Parawalla, 2008

Acrylic on canvas, 61 × 91 cm
Philippson Collection, inv. ENN1

Cat. 101

EUBEMA NAMPIJIN (ca. 1921–2013)
Ikara Rock Hole, 1997

Acrylic on canvas
Philippson Collection, inv. EUN1

Cat. 102

MAKINTI NAPANANGKA (ca. 1930–2011)
Untitled

Acrylic on canvas, 92 × 122 cm
Philippson Collection, inv. MN2

Cat. 103

KATHLEEN PETYARRE (ca. 1940–2018)
Mountain Devil Lizard, 2012

Acrylic on canvas, 197 × 198 cm
Philippson Collection, inv. KP6

Cat. 104 (p. 59)

KATHLEEN PETYARRE (ca. 1940–2018)
Mountain Devil Lizard, 2012

Acrylic on linen, 95 × 130 cm
Philippson Collection, inv. KP2

Cat. 105

LANCE PECK (ca. 1975)
Eagle Dreaming, 1997

Acrylic on canvas, 95 × 130 cm
Philippson Collection, inv. LAP1

Cat. 106 (p. 2)

WENTJA MORGAN NAPALTJARRI (ca. 1943)
Rockhole West of Kintore, 2015

Acrylic on canvas, 152 × 122 cm
Philippson Collection, inv. WMN1

Cat. 107

KATHLEEN PETYARRE (ca. 1940–2018)
Mountain Devil Lizard, 2009

Acrylic on canvas, 120 × 120 cm
Philippson Collection, inv. KP3

Cat. 108

MARC MENDELSON (1915–2013)
Spanish Landscape

Mixed media and oil on canvas,
162 × 114 cm
RMFAB, acquired in 1962, inv. 6966

Cat. 109

DOROTHY NAPANGARDI (ca. 1950–2013)
Mina Mina

Acrylic on canvas, 120 × 90 cm
Philippson Collection, inv. DN3

Cat. 110 (p. 64)

ABIE LOY KEMARRE (ca. 1972)
Woman's Body Painting, 2010

Acrylic on canvas, 152 × 60 cm
Philippson Collection, inv. ALK3

Cat. 111 (p. 63)

GLORIA TAMERRE PETYARRE (ca. 1942)
Wild Flowers and Medicine Leaves, 2005

Acrylic on canvas, 182 × 138 cm
Philippson Collection, inv. GTP6

Cat. 112

RONNIE TJAMPITJINPA (ca. 1943)
Tingari Dreaming, 2001

Acrylic on canvas, 132 × 97 cm
Philippson Collection, inv. RT2

Cat. 113

ESTHER GILES NAMPITJINPA (ca. 1948)
Punkilpirri

Acrylic on canvas, 102 × 112 cm
Philippson Collection, inv. EGN2

Cat. 114

GLORIA TAMERRE PETYARRE (ca. 1942)
Aknangkere, 1999

Acrylic on canvas, 91 × 122 cm
Philippson Collection, inv. GTP7

Cat. 115

MARC MENDELSON (1915–2013)
White and Black 6, 1954

Diluted oil on paper, 260 × 328 mm
RMFAB, donated by the artist, 1969,
inv. 7747

Cat. 116

MARC MENDELSON (1915–2013)
White and Black 5, 1954

Diluted oil on paper, 260 × 329 mm
RMFAB, donated by the artist, 1969,
inv. 7746

Cat. 117

MARC MENDELSON (1915–2013)
White and Black 3, 1954

Diluted oil on paper, 260 × 328 mm
RMFAB, donated by the artist, 1969,
inv. 7744

Cat. 118

MARC MENDELSON (1915–2013)
White and Black 4, 1954

Diluted oil on paper, 261 × 329 mm
RMFAB, donated by the artist, 1969,
inv. 7745

Cat. 119

GEORGE WARD TJUNGURRAYI (ca. 1945)
Tingari Cycle, 2009

Acrylic on canvas, 152 × 122 cm
Philippson Collection, inv. GWT1

Cat. 120 (p. 51)

SALLY GABORI (1924-2015)
Dibirdibi Country, 2010

Acrylic on canvas, 197 × 150 cm
Philippson Collection, inv. SG3

Cat. 121 (p. 65)

ABIE LOY KEMARRE (ca. 1972)
Untitled, 2004

Acrylic on linen, 151 × 153 cm
Philippson Collection, inv. ALK5

Cat. 122 (p. 53)

REGINA PILAWUK WILSON (ca. 1945)
Syaw (Fish net), 2002

Acrylic on canvas, 138 × 124 cm
Philippson Collection, inv. RPW1

Cat. 123

PRINCE OF WALES (MIDPUL) (ca. 1938–2002)
Body Marks, 2002

Acrylic on canvas, 91 × 76 cm
Philippson Collection, inv. POW1

Cat. 124 (p. 64)

ABIE LOY KEMARRE (ca. 1972)
Woman's Body Painting, 2010

Acrylic on linen, 152 × 60 cm
Philippson Collection, inv. ALK3

Cat. 125

ABIE LOY KEMARRE (ca. 1972)
Woman's Body Painting

Acrylic on canvas, 152 × 90 cm
Philippson Collection, inv. ALK6

Cat. 126

WALTER LEBLANC (1932–1986)
Twisting strings – MX 36, 1975

Strings sewn on canvas, all painted white and enclosed in a Plexiglas box, 96.5 × 96.5 cm
RMFAB, acquired in 1977, inv. 8912

Cat. 127 (p. 72)

JUDY WATSON NAPANGARDI (ca. 1925–2016)
Untitled

Acrylic on canvas, 98 × 73 cm
Philippson Collection, inv. JWN1a

Cat. 128

MINNIE PWERLE (1915–2006)
Aweley Atnwengerrp, 2005

Acrylic on canvas, 175 × 120 cm
Philippson Collection, inv. MP1

Cat. 129 (p. 80)

RUSTY PETERS (1935–2020)
Warrabayan, 2010

Natural pigment on canvas, 60 × 90 cm
Philippson Collection, inv. RP1

Cat. 130

RENÉ MAGRITTE (1898–1967)
The Apparition, 1928

Oil on canvas, 54 × 73 cm
Private collection, courtesy Brachot Gallery

Cat. 131 (p. 81)

PHYLLIS THOMAS (1933–2018)
Untitled, 2014

Natural pigment on canvas, 76 × 100 cm
Philippson Collection, inv. PT1

Cat. 132 (p. 77)

ROVER THOMAS JOOLAMA (1926–1998)
Untitled, 1990

Natural pigment on panel, 113 × 152 cm
Philippson Collection, inv. RTH2

Cat. 133 (p. 79)

ROVER THOMAS JOOLAMA (1926–1998)
Bubba Dog Dreaming, 1996

Natural pigment on canvas, 98 × 104 cm
Philippson Collection, inv. RTH1

Cat. 134 (p. 76)

RAMMEY RAMSEY (ca. 1935)
Warlawoon Country, 2007

Pigment on canvas, 150 × 180 cm
Philippson Collection, inv. RR1

This book accompanies the exhibition *Aboriginalities*, organised by the Royal Museums of Fine Arts of Belgium, Brussels, from 1 April until 1 August 2021.
It is published simultaneously in French, English and Dutch.

Publication
Author: Michel Draguet
General coordination and picture research: Fabrice Biasino
Redaction: Fabrice Biasino, with the support of Myriam Dom and Julie Stouffs
Translation: Paula Cook
Copy-editing: Kathie Berger
Graphic design and typesetting: Jurgen Persijn, N.N.
Printed and bound by die Keure, Bruges.

Royal Museums of Fine Arts of Belgium
Rue du Musée, 9
B-1000 Brussels
TEL. +32 (0)2 508 32 09
info@fine-arts-museum.be
www. fine-arts-museum.be

ISBN: 978-90-7701-331-1
Legal deposit: May 2021
D/2021/0324/3